OVER 25 CONTEMPORARY AND DELICATE CAKE
DECORATING DESIGNS

Elegant LACE CAKES

ZOE CLARK

David and Charles

www.stitchcraftcreate.co.uk

Contents

Introduction

Over the last five to ten years, lace has had an enormous influence in the fashion world, particularly in the wedding industry. This trend was enhanced by the 'vintage' phenomenon, which in turn made its way onto the cake scene. Those of you who are familiar with my work will know how much I love and am influenced by bridal lace, and many of the cakes in this book have been inspired by beautiful wedding dresses. But that's not completely it – if you look anywhere in the world of fashion at the moment you will still see lace featuring heavily on all kinds of garments, from tops and trousers to shoes and scarves. Lace prints are also incredibly popular with stationers and graphic designers; often seen in wedding invitation design.

Traditional lace cake design dates back to the late nineteenth century, when bakers would carefully pipe with royal icing to create extremely elaborate centrepieces for wedding cakes; a technique that required great skill and patience. Nowadays, as trends in sugarcraft evolve and new products are becoming easily available, we are able to transfer lace motifs onto cakes more quickly and simply using a variety of techniques and mediums. These include icing appliqués, brush embroidery, moulds, stencils, royal icing and the recent introduction of cake lace. The style of lace we see today is more contemporary, often teamed with beautiful textured fabrics or featuring isolated appliqués that add a touch of flair.

In this book I share my favourite methods and techniques for creating and replicating popular lace effects, and cover a range of skills for you to learn and adapt for your own designs. I would strongly recommend reading the front section first, which dives straight into the main lace techniques found in the projects. If you are a beginner, it is also a good idea to take a look at the end section in advance: this covers all the basic baking and decorating techniques, together with delicious recipes for cakes, cookies and mini cakes.

The twelve main projects are aimed mainly at beginner to intermediate level decorators, although a couple of the royal-iced cakes require slightly more skill. Each project features an alternative design – often a simplified version of the main cake – offering a great alternative if you are short of time or don't want to take on a big task. Don't forget, you can easily downsize many of the projects to cater for smaller numbers by reducing cake sizes or the number of tiers. The tables in the Recipes and Techniques section will help you to calculate the size you need for your event.

By no means do you have to replicate these designs exactly – they are there to inspire you and to showcase some of the many possibilities for creating your own lace textures and effects; whether you are hoping to match a particular fabric or pattern or just want to create something that looks amazing!

I hope you enjoy it!

Basic Tools and Equipment

The following checklists contain the basic equipment you will need for baking the cakes in this book, plus any handy tools for creative work. There are so many ways to achieve beautiful lace effects and I have listed my favourite tools and the essential equipment that can be used to create them. Any specific tools that are needed in addition to these basics can be found in the You Will Need lists at the start of each project.

BAKING BASICS

BAKEWARE
- **Cake tins** for baking cakes
- **Cupcake or muffin trays (pans)** for baking cupcakes
- **Baking tray (sheet)** for baking cookies
- **Wire racks** for cooling cakes

GENERAL EQUIPMENT
- **Electric mixer** for making cakes, buttercream and royal icing
- **Kitchen scales** for weighing out ingredients
- **Measuring spoons** for measuring small quantities
- **Mixing bowls** for mixing ingredients
- **Spatulas** for mixing and gently folding cake mixes
- **Greaseproof paper or baking (parchment) paper** for lining tins and to use under icing during preparation
- **Cling film (plastic wrap)** for covering icing to prevent drying out and for wrapping cookie dough
- **Large non-stick board** for rolling out icing (alternatively you may roll out icing on a workbench using a dusting of icing sugar to prevent sticking)
- **Non-slip mat** to put under the board to prevent it from slipping on the work surface
- **Pastry brush** for brushing sugar syrup and apricot masking spread or strained jam (jelly) onto cakes
- **Sharp knife or scalpel** for cutting and shaping icing
- **Large and small serrated knives** for carving and sculpting cakes
- **Cake leveller** for cutting even, level layers of sponge
- **Large and small palette knife** for applying buttercream and ganache
- **Icing or marzipan spacers** to give a guide to the thickness of icing and marzipan when rolling out
- **Icing smoothers** for smoothing icing
- **Spirit level** for checking that cakes are level when stacking them
- **Cake scraper** to scrape and smooth buttercream, ganache or royal icing; used in a similar way to a palette knife

CREATIVE TOOLS AND MATERIALS

- **Large and small non-stick rolling pins** for rolling out icing and marzipan

- **Turntable** for layering cakes

- **Double-sided tape** to attach ribbon around cakes and boards

- **Cocktail sticks (toothpicks) or cel sticks** for holding sugarpaste details in place

- **Edible glue** for sticking icing to icing

- **Edible pens** for marking details on sugarpaste

- **Cake-top marking template** for finding/marking the centre of cakes and marking where dowels should be placed.

- **Clear alcohol** for mixing into dust to paint on icing and for sticking icing to marzipan

- **Trex (white vegetable fat)** for greasing the board, pins and moulds

LACE ESSENTIALS

CUTTERS

- **Flower cutters** for cutting different types of decorative flowers from rolled-out flower (petal/gum) paste

- **Eyelet cutters** for cutting out petals and small holes from flower paste

- **Scroll cutters** for making decorative borders and details from flower paste

- **Strip cutters** for cutting thin strips from flower paste for borders and details, such as vines

- **Piping tubes (tips)** of different sizes for cutting out very small decorative holes from flower paste and using with a piping (pastry) bag to pipe royal icing

- **Punches** for cutting flowers and other shapes from wafer (rice) paper

DECORATING TOOLS

- **Stencils** a quick and easy way to add intricate detail to cakes and cookies (see Stenciling)

- **Ball tool** used with a foam pad to make indentations on flower paste details, such as cupping small flowers

- **Frilling tool** for frilling and softening edges

- **Dresden tool** for scoring pleats into icing

- **Brushes** for dusting lustre and smoothing piped royal icing

MOULDS AND MATS

- **Flower moulds** for quickly making floral details or adding texture to flower paste (see Moulds)

- **Lace moulds** for creating lace details from flower paste; you can use some or all of the design (see Moulds)

- **Plastic sleeve** for use with a template for piping work and to keep icing fresh while not in use

- **Cake lace mats** used with cake lace mixes to make large areas of lace designs for covering cakes, such as SugarVeil, Claire Bowman and Crystal Candy (see Suppliers)

Lace Techniques

INTRODUCTION TO FLOWER PASTE

In order to make sugar lace work as delicate and realistic as possible I like to use flower (petal/gum) paste for my appliqués, as it can be rolled incredibly thinly. Some brands of sugarpaste (rolled fondant) may also be suitable, as they are much firmer. You can also try mixing sugarpaste and flower paste together, but always be prepared to test the paste first; you may need to adjust or change the quantities in your icing.

APPLIQUÉS

The simplest technique for using flower paste is to apply floral shaped cut-outs to your cakes, randomly sticking them on so some touch and appear connected. I use this technique in the Gorgeous Guipure Lace cake, in which I connect the lace further by piping with royal icing (see Traditional Piping). The thinner the paste is rolled for your appliqués, the more elegant your pattern will be.

You can also use various tools to texture and shape your flower paste, such as the Dresden tool, ball tool and veining stick. Texture mats, moulds and embossers can be used to texture the flower paste before or after cutting out the shapes. Full instructions on using these tools are given in the step-by-step instructions with every project.

STRIP CUTTERS

Patterned border, frill and strip cutters are perfect for creating lacy trims around cakes. They can be used in a variety of ways around the centre, top and bottom of a tier, depending on the design. Scallop edge cutters are the most useful for lace work, as many lace fabrics – especially those found on wedding dresses – follow this shape.

You can texture the flower paste borders/trims by pressing them into lace moulds (see Moulds). Alternatively, for a more defined and interesting look you can try piping on top of a lace border with soft-peak royal icing (see Royal Icing); a technique that I use in the Little Blossom Laser Lace cake and Broderie Mini Cakes.

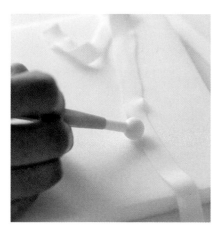

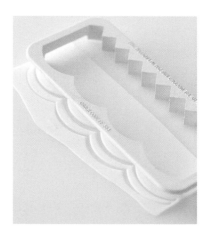

MOULDS

Silicone lace moulds are an absolute must-have for your decorator's tool kit, especially if you are hoping to create beautiful lacy designs without having to do any piping! They may seem a simple and easy option, but in fact there are correct techniques for using them and if these methods are not used, the elegant and delicate results you are hoping for will not be achieved. I use moulds to make the flowers in the Designed With Love and Gorgeous Guipure Lace cakes.

CHOOSING MOULDS

Moulds are fairly expensive to purchase, so just buy a few of your favourites at first, making sure they are versatile enough to be used in different ways, i.e. large enough to also be used as a texture mat and ideally featuring multiple, basic floral pieces within one mould. The quality of the mould and the material that they are made from is also important. In my opinion, you need to look for a very delicate and detailed design with a fairly shallow depth so the appliqué looks elegant when it is turned out.

USING MOULDS

I always use flower (petal/gum) paste in my moulds, as it is much firmer than sugarpaste (rolled fondant), but as with the appliqués, you could experiment with the material depending on the brand you are using. Follow these simple steps to use moulds to their best effect:

1 Brush pearl or matt lustre dust into the mould to prevent the flower paste from sticking. Vegetable shortening also works and may be needed on occasion, depending on the look and colour scheme you are going for.

2 Thinly roll the paste out first, then set it aside to dry out a little, especially if it's particularly sticky. I find that if you press the paste in straight away

it will still always stick, no matter how much dust or shortening you use! After a couple of minutes dust the mould, press in the paste and dust on top of the back of the paste – use cornflour (cornstarch) if you don't want to waste too much lustre dust.

3 Press the back of the mould fairly firmly on top. I tend to work rather cautiously for the first one, making sure the paste will release properly without pressing too hard.

4 While the paste is in the mould, you can usually tear away the excess paste from around the edge. If the moulds don't have a defined edge you will need to remove the paste first and then cut out the textured shape.

5 Remove the paste from the mould. If it sticks to either side, gently tease the paste away from the mould without stretching it. If you're not satisfied with the imprint, simply redust the mould press the paste back in again. It may have stretched a little, but just use your fingers to help it back into position. Press again and release and you should have a much better result.

6 As you continue and the rolled-out flower paste dries a little more, you will find moulding easier and the results will improve. However, the paste may start to become too dry, so you will need to cover it with a plastic sleeve between uses. Try to be as resourceful as possible when pressing the paste and always work from the outside in. You may not be able to save any leftover paste off-cuts, as they dry out quickly from dusting and after being exposed to the air.

DECORATING WITH ROYAL ICING

Edible stitching and embroidery with
royal icing is extremely traditional and this
delicate art usually requires a lot of patience
and dedication. I have tried to keep the
techniques I use as simple as possible in this
book so the beautifully piped stitching and
lace embroidery is easy to achieve. See
Decorating Techniques at the back of the book
for a royal icing recipe and advice on how to
make a piping bag and pipe with royal icing.

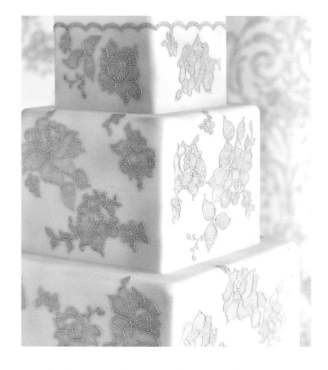

USING TEMPLATES
Before you get started, it's a good idea to choose
your pattern and know exactly where you want
the piping to be positioned. Once the design has
been selected, I prefer to use one of the following
two methods to transfer it onto the cake:

PENCIL TRANSFER METHOD
Before attempting to mark the pattern onto the
cake, it is very important that the icing is left to dry
for at least eight hours, otherwise it will dent easily
and the clean pencil lines could look messy. Bear
in mind that your pattern with be reversed when
it's transferred onto the cake: if you want it to look
exactly the same, you will need to reverse it first!

1 Trace your pattern (see Templates) onto some
greaseproof paper using a pencil – not too soft or
too hard. Place the paper onto the cake with the
pencil side against the icing and pin it in place so it
doesn't move about.

2 Lightly trace back over the pattern to transfer a light
pencil mark onto the icing, or prick though the pattern with
a needle to create a dotted line to follow. Take care not to
press too hard or smudge the pencil lines. You don't need
to follow the line continuously – just make little dashes.
Test the transfer has worked on a small section by peeling
back the template and realigning it when continuing.
Any visible pencil lines can be removed using a damp
paintbrush, cleaning it with water in-between uses.

CUSTOM EMBOSSER METHOD

Another way to transfer your design is to pipe your design onto a firm, thin piece of clear plastic and press it against the icing to emboss the pattern straight onto it. The sugarpaste (rolled fondant) needs to be soft and you will need to emboss the pattern as soon as the cakes or cookies are covered. You can also emboss actual lace samples, such as corded lace, straight onto the icing (see Elegant Embossed Cupcakes). Remember that the design will be reversed again when transferred onto the cake or cookie.

1 Place the plastic over the template and use a piping (pastry) bag fitted with a no. 1 piping tube (tip) and filled with soft-peak royal icing to trace over the design. The royal icing will need a good hour or so to dry out completely.

2 Carefully press the plastic against the icing to emboss the design. It's a good idea to practise this first to get the correct pressure if you haven't used this method before.

TRADITIONAL PIPING

Piped lacework is a highly traditional form of cake decorating: the earliest reference to royal icing dates back to the seventeenth century and piping work was made popular by bakers decorating wedding cakes in the late nineteenth century. Piping requires much patience, a lot of skill and correct use of technique, but the results can be simply breathtaking.

Traditional motifs and designs are often piped onto acetate or paper over templates, then left to dry before they are attached to the cake; a technique that I use to create the butterflies and daisies on the Royal-Iced Butterfly Garden cake. Lines need to be piped as accurately as possible to achieve a clean, delicate feel and it is helpful to have a damp paintbrush to hand to help push the icing into place if it's not perfect.

 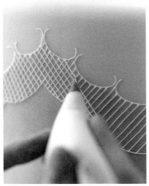

You can also pipe carefully straight onto the cake. Typical motifs include flowers, connecting dots, fleur-de-lis and scrolls. Swags, scallops, filigree and latticework are also traditional lace designs often featured in cake design, which you will see in the Hannah's Daisy Lace and Designed With Love cakes.

'BUMPY' PIPING

Trying to replicate lacy patterns by piping with royal icing is not as hard as it seems! If you look closely at lace embroidery you will see that it is in fact made up of lots of tiny stitches that give a slightly bumpy, textured appearance, rather than a perfectly smooth, continuous line. This makes it much easier to copy in royal icing.

To achieve this effect make sure you are using freshly made soft-peak royal icing and a fine piping tube (tip);

ideally a no. 0, unless the stitching is slightly thicker. Follow the markings along the sugarpaste with the tube almost scratching the icing or dotting against it. If you need to stop, just pick it back up again; the fact the line is slightly bumpy and uneven will disguise any breaks.

Zigzagging back and forth between lines and shapes can also be very effective at giving the appearance of lace stitching. Keep close to the surface, again, just about touching it as you move back and forth with the piping tube. Remember to keep breathing!

BRUSH EMBROIDERY

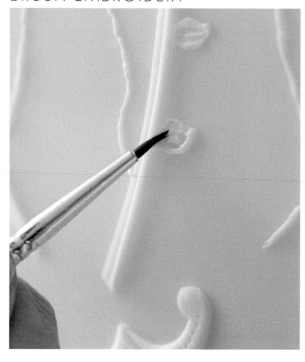

Brush embroidery is another traditional decorating technique with royal icing, although buttercream can also be used for this method. Like the bumpy stitching technique, it's not as hard as it seems, and although a steady hand is not essential, you do need to work neatly and methodically in order to achieve a pretty result.

I like to use a no. 1.5 or 2 piping tube (tip) and soft-peak royal icing when working on lace brush embroidery, as the motifs are fairly small and the outlines quite wavy. If the tube is too big you will have too much icing; at the same time if the tube is too small you won't have enough icing to brush, so make sure you adjust your tube according to your design.

1 Pipe a section of the outline using a piping (pastry) bag with a no. 1.5 or 2 tip, filled with soft-peak royal icing.

2 Using a damp brush, work the icing inwards from the outer top edge of the line. You can experiment with how far you drag the icing in, depending on the look you want to create or the piece of lace you are copying; more pressure and longer brush strokes means the icing will come further into the shape.

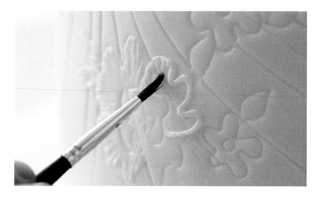

3 Continue piping bit by bit all the way around the shape, brushing the icing down in-between. Once you have completed the entire shape and it has had time to dry, start working on the inside details. If the icing isn't quite dry on the outside, the inside is likely to run and the lines will not be defined.

OVER-PIPING AND OUTLINING

Cord lace, also known as Alençon Lace, is one of the most popular types of modern lace we see on dresses today and is formed by outlining lace details with a heavier stitch or cord (see Contemporary Corded Lace). If you look closely at this type of lace, you will see that the outline does not run perfectly around the outside, so when you copy this, try to follow the same style.

CAKE LACE

In the last few years we have seen the introduction and amazing growth in popularity of cake lace; a fairly ground-breaking material that enables delicate and detailed edible pieces of lace to be produced with flexible properties so they can be wrapped around cakes. The process is quick and the technique is very easy to do, which means impressive and decorative designs can be achieved in a no time.

CAKE LACE MIXES AND MATS

Since the original SugarVeil line, there are now quite a few different products available on the market, and they each come with their own 'mat' designs and cake lace mixes. As each product has its own recipe – and they are all slightly different – I haven't included any instructions on how to mix the cake lace here: simply follow the manufacturer's instructions. Most mixes are made with a powder and water, and usually the addition of a type of glycerine to make the icing stay flexible. Some mixes also come ready-made; simply spread the mixture straight from the tub!

Cake lace mats and mixes are available to buy separately – I tend to always use one type of cake lace mix for every type of mat! I like the Claire Bowman brand because it's British and I'm happy with the results every time. Claire also produces some great online tutorials to demonstrate how the products work; a great resource for beginners. I also like to use the SugarVeil mats, which are very delicate, and Crystal Candy, who make incredibly pretty designs.

PEARLIZED CAKE LACE MIXES

Pearlized mixes are great to use on decorations that you wish to stand out from the surface of the cake or cookie, such as the butterflies on the Cake Lace Cupcakes. Some pearlized colours, such as gold and silver, come ready-made. However, pearlized mixes are usually much more brittle, so if you're hoping to bend them around your cake you would need a second coat of the plain mix to give the cake lace some flexibility. Ideally, the colour of the second coat should match the colour of your cake or cookie.

USING CAKE LACE

1 To create the lace pieces, spread the mix into the moulds/mats using a spatula or spreader. Work in different directions to remove any air bubbles and make sure the mix fills in every detail in the design. When you've completely covered the mat, clean the spreader and give one final sweep over the top to clean up any mix that may have smudged onto the top of the mat, outside of the embossed design.

2 Now leave the lace to dry. At room temperature this will take anything from four hours to overnight, depending on the size of the details and the humidity of the atmosphere. Alternatively, you can place the mat in a low oven (80°C/180°F) for about 15–20 minutes. If you are drying out the lace in the oven, take care not to overcook it as this will make it brittle.

3 For some designs you might like to add a second coat of the mix to make the cake lace stronger, particularly if the design is very delicate. After the first drying, spread more mix into the mould and return it to the oven, or air-dry it as before.

4 To test if the lace is ready, peel away a small corner to see if it releases. For large cake lace mats, turn the mat upside down, hold the spreader on the lace, and peel the mat back. If you are using smaller pieces of lace, you can just peel them out using your fingers.

5 Store the lace on a tray between sheets of greaseproof paper until you are ready to use them. If you are in a dry climate you can also wrap the lace in plastic to prevent it from drying out. In humid, cold and damp climates the lace can become soft and sticky after it has initially dried out. You can carefully return it to the oven on some greaseproof paper to dry it out again before use; just keep an eye on it.

6 To stick the cake lace to the sugarpaste you can either brush the cake or cookie with water or clear alcohol or use a small amount of edible glue on the back of the cake lace. I usually use the first method for larger pieces and the second for smaller pieces.

COLOURING CAKE LACE

Cake lace can be coloured by adding paste or gel food colourings towards the end of the mixing stage, although I would only make pale colours in this way. For darker colours, I usually purchase pre-coloured mixes, such as red and black. You can also airbrush the lace to achieve a particular shade, building up the colour gradually so the cake lace doesn't dissolve.

STENCILLING

Cake lace stencils are another quick and simple way to create intricate lace decorations, and can be completely customized to match a particular lace. There is a huge variety of stencils now available and a number of ways you can use them to decorate your cakes.

USING STENCILS

The most common way of using stencils is to spread a thin layer of royal icing (see Royal Icing) straight over the top of the design, using a palette knife to transfer it onto the icing. You can cover areas of the stencil with masking tape to include only the details you require.

As well as simply spreading on the icing, it is also nice to texture it. For the Ornate Stencil Lace cake, I brush down the icing across the stencil using a damp, medium-sized

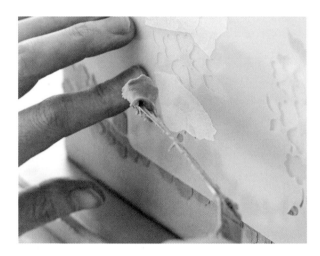

dusting brush to try to create more of an embroidered appearance. Alternatively, you can place netting or tulle up in front of the stencil so the icing takes on this lighter textured appearance as it transfers onto the cake.

Finally, carefully peel off the stencil to reveal the pattern underneath and use a fine paintbrush to neaten up any stray pieces of icing, particularly at the ends. Always wash and dry your stencil thoroughly between uses. Additional piped details, such as dots, leaves and scallop lines, can really lift the design, along with sequin and pearl embellishments (see Embellishments).

WAFER PAPER TECHNIQUES

Wafer paper, or rice paper as some people call it, has become an extremely fashionable material to use in cake decoration in the last couple of years. It lends itself really well to delicate embellishments with its incredibly light, almost transparent form.

By crossing over into the world of papercrafts, we can use the many beautiful lacy trim and flower punches available to create gorgeous edible paper lace decorations for our cakes. I touch upon this technique in the Delicate Doily Art cakes, which use wafer paper for borders and trims, flower decorations and even an elaborate doily ball topper.

Wafer paper is also a great material to use for quick and easy flower decorations. Simply punch out little flowers, or make your own shapes to create texture and interest. Three-dimensional flowers and corsages are also quick to make and are a great alternative to sugar flowers, as you will see in the Contemporary Corded Lace design.

EMBELLISHMENTS

The addition of other decorative elements will add interest to your design, especially if you are trying to copy a particular lace. I like to use embellishments, such as pearl and silver dragées, edible glitter and edible sequins, to add extra sparkle. Bows, satin ribbons and corsages are also strongly associated with lace and bridal wear and can bring an elegant finishing touch to a cake.

EDIBLE SEQUINS

You can either buy ready-made edible sequins or make your own by cutting out tiny circles with very small cutters or larger round piping tubes (tips), shaping them with a ball tool so they cup upwards slightly in the middle, and brushing them with pearl lustre dust. You can also make edible sequins using Claire Bowman's sequin mat and cake lace mix product (see Cake Lace), which I use in the Designed With Love cake.

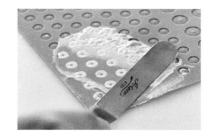

COLOUR AND COLOURINGS

The use and choice of colour is extremely important and can really change the look of a design, especially when it comes to 'Elegant Lace Cakes'! My preference is for white- or ivory-coloured lace on top of a pale-coloured background so the colour change is subtle, as you would see on a typical wedding dress. However, it is much more difficult to see the detail in a cake with little colour contrast from afar – something to think about when you are designing your cake. At the other end of the spectrum, black lace can look really beautiful, especially against neutral colours, such as white, silver and gold. Personally, I'm not too keen on anything in-between, but that's up to you and the recipient of your cake to decide!

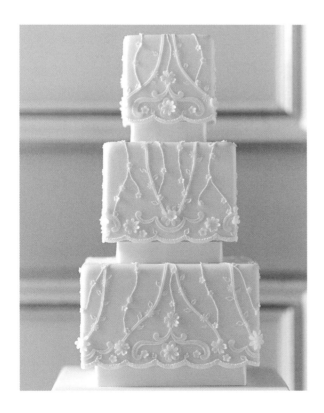

Although many of the designs in this book are in paler shades, I include some cakes in different colours to inspire you, such as Lace, Ruffles and Ribbons, Royal-Iced Butterfly Garden and Hannah's Daisy Lace. You don't have to stop at changing the colour of your lace applications, but you can also experiment with the colour of the background or use different colours for the separate lace elements. For example, the outlines could be a different colour to stand out, or you could use one colour for the floral elements and another for the swirls and leaves. You can also add colour in other ways, such as in the ribbons and flower embellishments.

DRY DUSTING AND LUSTRING

AIRBRUSHING AND SPRAYING

PAINTING

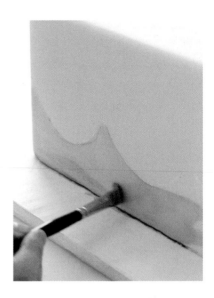

Using a large flat brush you can dust either matt powder or lustre straight onto the sugarpaste to give it some shine. I use this technique on the Ornate Stencil Lace cake. Ideally, the icing should have been left to dry and harden for at least eight hours or overnight before doing this, otherwise you can dent it. I like to build up colour rather than brushing it on too heavily initially – if you have too much dust on the brush you can make the icing look really streaky. Also, the softer the brush you use; the less likely you are to have a streaky finish. Take more care when dusting on colours that contrast with the base colour.

Airbrushing is becoming more and more popular, and these days the average 'semi-professional cake decorator' or keen hobbyist is quite likely to own an airbrush! While it's not something I use everyday I really like to create subtle colour tones and pearlized effects using my airbrush, as I find the result really interesting, especially with the lace overlays.

Airbrushes are not difficult to use and once you have mastered the art you will be able to add additional colour effects to your cakes, as I will show in the Delicate Doily Art cake. You can also find many tutorials online to help you if you are just starting out. If you don't have an airbrush, you can use a variety of colour sprays, which are widely available from cake decorating stores. However, the drawback of using sprays is that you don't have much control over the amount that comes out, so very subtle colouring becomes more difficult.

You can also create a really striking pearlized effect by painting edible dust or airbrush paint straight from the bottle onto the sugarpaste; a technique that I use for the Ornate Stencil Lace cake. This gives an interesting 'brushed' appearance to the surface and is a huge trend at the moment.

If you are using dust, mix it with a fair amount of very high alcohol content liquid and brush it onto the cake in one direction using a large dusting brush. Apply only a thin coat at first, and then brush over the surface with a large dry dusting brush. Allow it to dry and then paint a second coat, and maybe a third as well if the colour is not as strong as you are hoping for.

Once dry, you can also go over everything again with a dry dust and a big fluffy brush to blend in any streaks.

Delicate Doily Art

I was inspired by simple paper doilies to create this duo of elegantly decorated tiered cakes. I love the effect of laser cutting and die-cutting to create patterned borders that are both interesting and delicate. Here I've used paper punches to make my own doily stencils, but you could use real doilies instead. The theme perfectly combines the modern art of airbrushing with the growing popularity of wafer paper decorations. Experiment by mixing and matching the designs and using different punches to create your own unique results.

YOU WILL NEED

MATERIALS

For the four-tier cake:

- 10cm (4in); 15cm (6in); 20cm (8in); and 25cm (10in) round cakes, each approximately 10–11.5cm (4–4½in) deep (see Cake Recipes), iced in white sugarpaste (rolled fondant) ideally 24 hours in advance (see Covering with Sugarpaste)
- 28cm (11in) round cake drum iced in white sugarpaste at least 24 hours in advance (see Icing Cake Boards)
- A4 wafer (rice) paper: 3 sheets of white; 2 sheets of green; (3 sheets of simple satin ribbon or coloured paper – optional)

For the two-tier cake:

- 13cm (5in) round, 10cm (4in) deep; and 18cm (7in) round, 13cm (5in) deep cakes (see Cake Recipes), both iced in white sugarpaste ideally 24 hours in advance (see Covering with Sugarpaste)
- 23cm (9in) cake drum iced in white sugarpaste at least 24 hours in advance (see Icing Cake Boards)
- A4 wafer (rice) paper: 4 sheets of white, 3 of sheets of blue; (3 sheets of simple satin ribbon or coloured paper – optional)

For both cakes:

- Airbrush paint colours: Sky Blue, Sage Green (Dinky Doodle) or edible sprays
- 25g (1oz) white flower (petal/gum) paste
- 60ml (4 tbsp) royal icing (see Royal Icing)

EQUIPMENT

- Eyelet doily circle edge punch starter kit and Doily lace trim deep edge punch (Martha Stewart Crafts)
- Paper (ideally A3 size)
- Scissors or scalpel
- Cutting board or appropriate surface to cut on
- Pins
- Airbrush
- 12 dowels cut to size of each tier (see Assembling Tiered Cakes)
- Petal template (see Templates)
- 1.5cm (⅝in) circle cutter
- 1.8m (2yd) length of 1.5cm (⅝in) blue satin ribbon

FOUR-TIER CAKE

1 Cut out the paper doilies using the circle edge punch, following the manufacturer's instructions. You will need two doilies of each size: 15cm (6in), 20cm (8in), 25cm (10in) and 30cm (12in) **(A)**.

2 Use a ruler to mark a line slightly off-centre across each doily. Cut along the line using scissors or a scalpel on a cutting board to give you segments of varying sizes **(B)**. Carefully attach the segments around each tier with pins. The 30cm (12in) doilies are to be positioned on the bottom 25cm (10in) tier; the 25cm (10in) doilies on the second 20cm (8in) tier and so on, so you achieve a gradient in size as you go up the cake. You will only fit two pieces of doily on the top tier if you want them to come fairly high up the sides of the cake; otherwise cut them shorter in order to fit three pieces on.

3 Fill your airbrush with blue paint, hold it about 20cm (8in) from the cake and carefully spray lightly around the edges and hole details of each doily **(C)** (see Airbrushing and Spraying). Parts of the design can be stronger in colour, however you will need the changes to look subtle. Spray each tier and then spray around the outer edge of the cake drum. If you don't have an airbrush, use edible sprays instead.

4 Clean out your airbrush and fill it with green paint. Now go over parts of each tier using this new colour, ensuring that the blue background still shows through **(D)**. Repeat for the base board.

5 Remove all the pins and paper doilies. Dowel and assemble the cake tiers onto the base board (see Assembling Tiered Cakes).

6 To make the trim around the bottom of each tier use the lace trim punch to cut strips from green wafer paper **(E)** (see Wafer Paper Techniques). Cut each strip in half down the centre with a ruler and scalpel or scissors on your cutting surface **(F)**.

7 Attach the wafer paper trim to the cake using a minimal amount of edible glue so the paper doesn't dissolve. Try to join the pieces as neatly and invisibly as possible. If you don't have wafer paper, you can substitute this for simple satin ribbon or coloured paper.

8 To make the flower decorations start by cutting out two 15cm (6in) and two 20cm (8in) doilies from white wafer paper using the circle edge punch. Make use of all the paper – you can cut out half doilies from any off-cuts.

Tip

A3 paper is ideal, but if you only have A4 paper you can cut out parts of the doilies for the larger sizes. Try different thicknesses and types of paper, as some cut better than others.

A

B

C

D

E

F

Tip

I like to have the pitted side of the rice paper facing out, as I think it looks prettier!

9 Use the template (see Templates) to cut out the petal shapes from the doilies (**G**). You will need five petals for each flower. Cut a slit a third of the way up the base of each petal. Brush a small amount of edible glue on one side of the slit and overlap the end of the petal (**H**). Repeat with all five petals.

10 Thinly roll out the white flower paste and cut out ten circles with the circle cutter. One at a time, attach five petals onto five of the flower paste discs (**I**). Space the petals evenly, overlapping them as you go. You can try tucking the last petal under the first, but if it is too stuck down simply sit it over the top.

11 Use any off-cuts from the doilies to make the flower centres. Place the circle cutter on top of the flower detail at the edge of a doily and cut around it using a scalpel or scissors (**J**). Lightly glue the paper centres onto the five remaining flower paste discs. Attach the centres to the flowers and allow them to dry briefly before securing them onto the cake with some royal icing. They should stick fairly quickly, as they are very light. Finish by securing satin ribbon around the base board (see Securing Ribbon Around Cakes and Boards).

TWO-TIER CAKE

1 Start by cutting out paper strips with the lace trim punch to use as stencils around the 13cm (5in) and 18cm (7in) tiers. The strips must be long enough to wrap once around the top tier and twice around the bottom tier – approximately 165cm (65in) in total. Carefully pin the strips to the cakes, making sure they are all horizontal and parallel to the top and bottom of the cake.

2 Airbrush the cakes, first with the green paint then add accents with the blue (see Step 4, Four-Tier Cake). Concentrate the paint mainly around the strips, making sure the spray tapers off evenly. Spray around the edge of the base board, then assemble the tiers onto it (see Assembling Tiered Cakes).

3 To make the doily ball topper, cut out ten 15cm (6in) doilies from wafer paper using the circle edge punch (see Wafer Paper Techniques). Make use of the entire A4 wafer paper sheet: you will get one full and one half doily

from each one. Cut each doily in half exactly and form them into a cone, overlapping the two end scallops so they line up and carefully sticking them together with a minimal amount of edible glue.

4 Roughly cut out two circles from the wafer paper off-cuts, about 4cm (1½in) in diameter. Assemble ten cones onto one circle (using seven cones for the initial base and filling in with three on top) then stick the other ten cones onto the other circle in the same way (**K**). Allow both pieces to dry briefly before gluing them together to form a ball. Set aside to dry completely.

5 To make the scallop border for the base of the tiers cut the outer sections from wafer paper of any size using the circle edge. Trim the pieces across each scallop so they are identical with a flat edge and stick them around the cake with a small amount of edible glue. Finish by securing satin ribbon around the base board (see Securing Ribbon Around Cakes and Boards).

Always be on the lookout for inspiration. The idea for this cake came from a tutorial for a doily ball topper that I found via Patricia Zapata's blog and decided to make edible!

Doily Delights Cupcakes

These sweet cupcakes, simply topped with wafer paper bows cut using the lace trim punch, perfectly continue the doily theme. Or why not use the circle edge punch to create delicately detailed cupcake wrappers to jazz up some simple swirl-topped cupcakes?

YOU'LL ALSO NEED
- Cupcakes (see Baking Cupcakes) in white cases (liners) topped with a disc of white, pale blue and pale green sugarpaste (rolled fondant), cut using a fluted round cutter (see Covering Cupcakes with Sugarpaste)
- Cupcakes topped with buttercream swirls, piped using a large piping (pastry) bag and a large plain round piping tube (tip)
- Wafer (rice) paper: white; pale green; pale blue
- Thin coloured card

BOW-TOPPED CUPCAKES
To make the bows, first cut a strip of wafer paper using the lace trim punch (it should be nine scallops long). Trim the last scallop off each end and the centre to make these areas slightly thinner. Fold the ends into the centre – one on top of the other – and secure with edible glue **(A)**. Cut a 7cm (2¾in) strip for around the centre and glue in place. Cut two tails and glue them onto the cupcake, before sticking the bow on top.

CUPCAKES IN DOILY WRAPPERS
To make the cupcake wrappers, simply cut out a section of thin card measuring eight scallops wide from a 30cm (12in) doily. Cut a line parallel to the outer edge, about 7.5cm (3in) in, using a plate or cake board about 30cm (12in) in diameter to help you. Finally, stick the two ends of the wrapper together using a small piece of tape or pretty sticker.

A

Beautiful Broderie Anglaise

I absolutely love the fresh, simplistic look of broderie anglaise, or 'English embroidery' as it translates. The combination of cut out holes and needlework gives fabric an interesting look and texture, which can easily be replicated in sugar. Here I covered each tier with yellow sugarpaste before re-covering with white and cutting out the flower details. The main 'embroidery' around the cutwork is made using flower paste that is textured for a stitch effect. Experiment with any accent colour to make the detail stand out, or choose pure white for a clean, delicate style.

YOU WILL NEED

MATERIALS

- 10cm (4in) round, 11.5cm (4½in) deep; 18cm (7in) round, 12cm (4¾in) deep; and 25cm (10in) round, 13cm (5in) deep cakes (see Cake Recipes), each iced in a thin layer of pale yellow sugarpaste (rolled fondant) leaving a fairly sharp edge, at least 24 hours in advance (see Covering with Sugarpaste)
- One 33cm (13in) round cake drum iced in white sugarpaste at least 24 hours in advance (see Icing Cake Boards)
- 2kg (4lb 8oz) white sugarpaste
- 100g (3½oz) white flower (petal/gum) paste
- Pearl lustre dust
- Quarter quantity of royal icing (see Royal Icing Recipe)
- Clear alcohol or lemon extract

EQUIPMENT

- Circle cutters: 1cm (³⁄₈in); 1.3cm (½in); 2cm (¾in)
- Teardrop/petal cutters: 1.8cm (⅝in); 3cm (1¼in)
- Seven hollow dowels cut to size of each tier (see Assembling Tiered Cakes)
- Multi-flower veiner (FMM)
- Large soft dusting brush
- Small piping (pastry) bag fitted with no. 1.5 piping tube (tip)
- Fine paintbrush
- 110cm (44in) length of 1.5cm (⅝in) white satin ribbon

1 Coat the 10cm (4in) round cake in a small amount of trex (white fat/vegetable shortening) before covering it with a thin layer of white sugarpaste. Use the 2cm (¾in) circle cutter to lightly mark the centre of each flower onto the cake: there are four flowers around the 10cm (4in) tier. Cut out the centres with the 1cm (⅜in) cutter.

2 Use the smaller teardrop/petal cutter to cut out eight petals around each centre (A). To achieve an even distribution, start by cutting out opposite petals then divide each side in half and cut out the petals in-between. Leave a small gap between the centre and each petal point and use a small knife or cocktail stick (toothpick) to tease out the icing (B).

3 Use the 1.3cm (½in) cutter randomly to cut out extra circles around the cake, spacing them about 4–5cm (1½–2in) apart.

4 Repeat this process (Steps 1–4) to cut out six flowers on the 18cm (7in) tier and nine flowers on the 25cm (10in) tier. Cut the holes so they come up over the edge of the tiers without disappearing beneath the tier above.

5 Dowel and assemble the three tiers on top of the prepared cake drum (see Assembling Tiered Cakes).

6 For the main 'embroidery' around the cutwork, thinly roll out the flower paste and use the 3cm (1¼in) teardrop/petal cutter to cut out enough petals for all the flowers on the cake, re-rolling the paste if necessary.

7 Use the dusting brush to dust the flower veiner fairly heavily on both sides with pearl lustre and press each petal individually into the mould (see Moulds). Use the smaller teardrop/petal cutter to cut out the centre of each petal, leaving a stitched border (C). Attach the borders around each petal using a small amount of edible glue.

8 Thinly roll out some more white flower paste and cut out circles with the 2cm (¾in) cutter. Press the paste into the flower veiner, using more pearl lustre, then remove the centre with the 1.3cm (½in) cutter (D). Attach the textured round borders around the centres and extra circles.

9 Fill the piping bag with soft-peak royal icing and pipe around the flower centres and extra circles. Before the icing dries, pat it down with a damp fine paintbrush to give it an embroidered texture (see Brush Embroidery) (E).

10 Mix a small amount of pearl lustre dust with clear alcohol or lemon extract and paint over the piped outlines. Finish by securing satin ribbon around the base board (see Securing Ribbon Around Cakes and Boards).

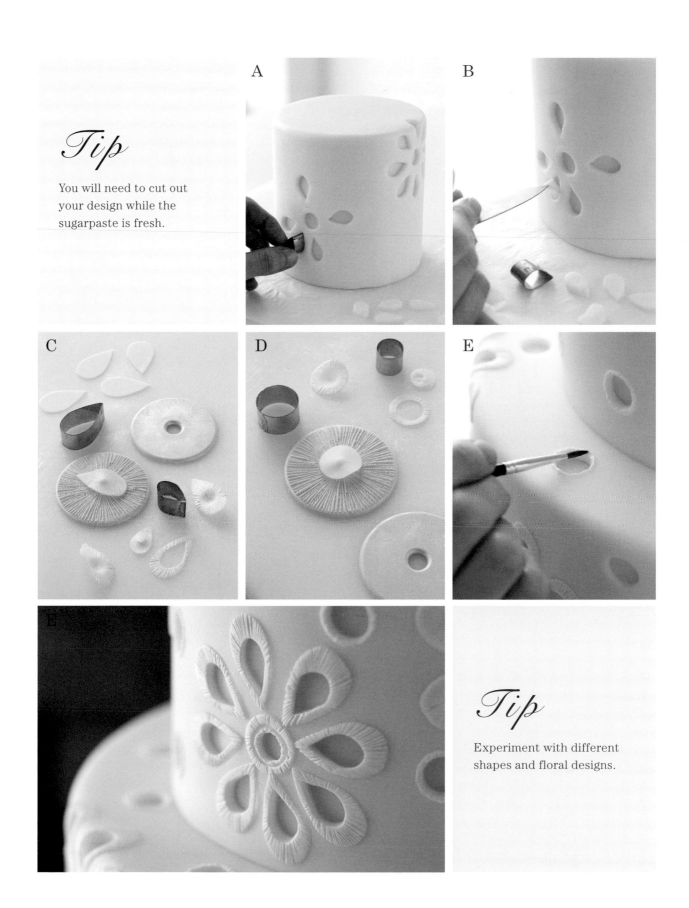

Tip

You will need to cut out
your design while the
sugarpaste is fresh.

C

D

E

E

Tip

Experiment with different
shapes and floral designs.

Broderie Mini Cakes

The beautiful scalloped-edge border and delicate blossom topper continue the broderie anglaise theme of this pale yellow mini cake design, which is enhanced with cut out flowers and piping details. Make the blossom toppers first to allow for plenty of drying time.

YOU'LL ALSO NEED

- 5cm (2in) round mini cakes (see Mini Cakes) iced in pale yellow sugarpaste (rolled fondant)
- White flower (petal/gum) paste
- Blossom cutters: 6cm (2³⁄₈in); 2.5cm (1in)
- Eyelet cutters: single petal; five-petal (PME)
- Flower former or apple tray
- Scallop edge strip cutter (FMM)
- No. 7 piping tube (tip) (Wilton) or round eyelet cutter (PME)
- Piping (pastry) bag fitted with a no. 1 piping tube filled with soft-peak royal icing (see Royal Icing Recipe)

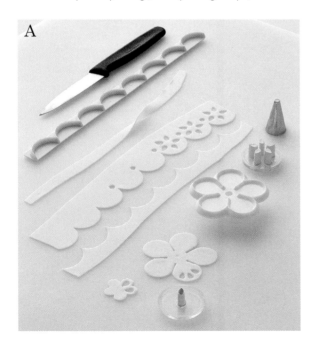

A

BLOSSOM TOPPER

Roll out some white flower paste to 1mm (¹⁄₃₂in) thick. Cut out the base flower using the larger blossom cutter and the centre with the smaller blossom cutter. Use the single petal eyelet cutter to take out holes around the petals of both pieces **(A)**. Set the flowers aside to dry separately using a slightly curved flower former or apple tray to cup them in position.

SCALLOP BORDER

Thinly roll out some more white flower paste to 23 x 5cm (9 x 2in). Cut a scallop edge along one side of the paste with the strip cutter. Use the eyelet cutter to cut out five-petal flowers in-between the arches all the way along the paste. Then cut out a small hole in-between each flower with the no. 7 piping tube or a round eyelet cutter **(A)**.

Cut a straight edge parallel to the scallop edge with a sharp knife. Wrap the band around the base of the mini cake and secure with edible glue, then trim the ends so they sit neatly together.

FINISHING TOUCHES

Use the piping bag with no. 1 tube to carefully pipe soft-peak royal icing around the scallop edges, petals and cut out holes. Now pipe around the outside of the blossoms on the flower. When the flower is completely dry, stick the smaller blossom in the centre of the larger blossom with royal icing and attach the flower onto the cake using more royal icing.

Hannah's Daisy Lace

Piped lines and daisies form the delightful decoration on this five-tier pastel design, inspired by another beautiful and unique wedding dress worn by one of my most hardworking employees, Hannah. The dress was originally her mother's – worn over thirty years ago – and I love the fact that the lace design still works so well today. The darker pink areas add interest and allow the pure white icing to stand out even more. With the correct techniques and plenty of patience, this design is achievable for anyone with basic piping skills.

YOU WILL NEED

MATERIALS

- 10cm (4in) round, 9.5cm (3¾in) deep; 15cm (6in) round, 10cm (4in) deep; 20cm (8in) round, 13cm (5in) deep; 25cm (10in) round, 15cm (6in) deep; and 33cm (13in) round, 11cm (4¼in) deep cakes (see Cake Recipes) all iced in pale pink sugarpaste (rolled fondant) (I mixed dusky pink into ivory icing) at least 24 hours in advance (see Covering with Sugarpaste)
- One 40cm (16in) cake drum iced in pale pink sugarpaste (see Icing Cake Boards) and stuck onto another 40cm (16in) cake drum
- Edible dust colours: dusky pink; cream
- One quantity of royal icing (see Royal Icing Recipe)

EQUIPMENT

- Basic design templates (see Templates)
- Pins
- Pencil
- Large soft dusting brush
- Small piping (pastry) bags
- Piping tubes (tips): nos. 0 and 1.5
- Fine paintbrush
- Scriber
- Dowels cut to size of each tier (see Assembling Tiered Cakes)
- 33cm (13in) length of 2.5cm (1in) satin ribbon plus lace trim (optional)

Dainty Daisy Lace Cookies

These square cookies continue the daisy theme with their dainty flowers and intricate lattice work. I reversed the colour scheme, this time piping a vibrant shade of pink icing onto white. Piping onto a flat surface from above is much easier than onto the side of a cake, so these are great for beginners.

YOU'LL ALSO NEED
- 6cm (2½in) square cookies (see Baking Cookies) iced in white royal icing (see Royal-Iced Cookies)
- Piping (pastry) bags fitted with no. 0 and 1.5 tubes (tips) filled with pink (Sugarflair Claret paste colour) soft-peak royal icing (see Royal Icing Recipe)

DAISY BORDER COOKIES
First pipe one square inside another using a piping bag fitted with a no. 0 tube (see Traditional Piping). Change to the no. 1.5 tube and pipe the daisies (see Step 7, Hannah's Daisy Lace) around the outside of the cookie. To achieve an even pattern, pipe the flowers on the corners first, then the central flowers on each side and finally fill in-between.

Next pipe on the connecting lines between the square border lines with the no. 0 tube. Change back to the no. 1.5 tube and thicken and brush down the inside square border. Pipe the hollow centre flower in the centre of the cookie, then add the vines and leaves (see Step 8, Hannah's Daisy Lace).

LATTICE COOKIES
Start by piping a 'c' scroll line across one corner. Next pipe a curved scallop border almost across the centre diagonal of the cookie, in line with the 'c' scroll. Pipe a second line to the curved scallop, then pipe the little circles in-between.

Next pipe on the lattice work (see Step 12, Hannah's Daisy Lace). Use the no. 1.5 tube to thicken the 'c' scroll and brush the icing down with a damp paintbrush. Finish by adding the flower, leaf and 'fleur-de-lis' embellishments, using the same techniques as for the main cake.

Designed With Love

This enchanting romantic tiered cake was inspired by one of my favourite bridal designers, Claire Pettibone. She combines vintage, ethereal detail with a modern feel in her couture wedding gowns: often bringing together different fabrics, textures and styles, and adding sewn-on appliqués for whimsical effect. In the same way, I have used a number of techniques and mediums in the creation of this cake, including airbrushing and piping. I also added detail with wafer paper leaves, floral lace appliqués, and — for a sparkling finishing touch — edible sequins and tiny pearls.

YOU WILL NEED

MATERIALS

- 9cm (3½in) round, 10cm (4in) deep; 13cm (5in) round, 11.5cm (4½in) deep; 18cm (7in) round, 13cm (5in) deep; and 23cm (9in) round, 14cm (5½in) deep cakes (see Cake Recipes), all iced in pale coffee-coloured sugarpaste (rolled fondant) (see Covering with Sugarpaste)
- 30cm (12in) cake board covered in pale coffee-coloured sugarpaste (see Icing Cake Boards)
- Pearl airbrush paint or edible spray
- Quarter quantity of soft-peak royal icing (see Royal Icing Recipe)
- 3 sheets of A4 wafer (rice) paper
- Piping gel
- Pearl lustre dust
- Clear alcohol or lemon extract
- Flower (petal/gum) paste: 50g (1¾oz) each of cream, very pale brown and white
- Silver sequins made with a sequin mould and cake lace mix (Claire Bowman) or shop-bought edible sequins (see Edible Sequins)
- 20g (¾oz) pale coffee-coloured sugarpaste
- Tiny pearl dragees

EQUIPMENT

- 5 × 75cm (2 × 30in) piece of greaseproof paper
- Airbrush (optional)
- Seven pieces of hollow dowel cut to size for the 23cm (9in) and 18cm (7in) tiers (see Assembling Tiered Cakes)
- Three pieces of 'bubble tea' straws or thin dowels cut to size for the 13cm (5in) tier
- Scriber
- Small piping (pastry) bag fitted with no.1 tube (tip)
- Flower and leaf template (see Templates)
- Blossom punch
- Appliqué Lace moulds: small blossom; mini daisy single; floral V spray (Decorate The Cake)
- 1.25m (1³⁄₈yd) length of 1.5cm (⁵⁄₈in) white satin ribbon

1 Wrap the greaseproof paper around the bottom of the 23cm (9in) cake and spray the rest of the tier with pearl airbrush paint or edible spray (see Airbrushing and Spraying). Now spray the top three tiers, gently building up colour by covering the surface in one layer, allowing it to dry and then spraying again. Repeat three times and then remove the greaseproof paper from the bottom tier.

2 Dowel and assemble the cake tiers onto the base board (see Assembling Tiered Cakes). To support the smaller tier use either bubble tea straws or thin dowels cut to size.

3 Use a scriber to mark points on the pearl edge for the border around the bottom tier. The points should alternate between 2.5cm (1in) and 4cm (1½in) apart.

4 Fill the piping bag with soft-peak royal icing and pipe lines to connect the points: straight lines to connect the marks that are 2.5cm (1in) apart and upward 'V' lines for the marks that are 4cm (1½in) apart (see Traditional Piping). If the pattern doesn't meet up perfectly at the back of the cake, try to space it evenly across the last few points **(A)**.

5 Place a piece of wafer paper over the flower template (see Templates) with the dimpled/rough side facing out and trace the outline and inner lines using a scriber **(B)**. Cut out the flower using scissors. Repeat to make eight flowers and attach them onto the cake with some piping gel. You should have three flowers on the 23cm (9in) tier, three on the 18cm (7in) tier and one each on the top two tiers, all evenly spaced apart.

6 Mark in the vines using the scriber **(C)**. I repeated the same design for the flowers on each tier (the pattern is repeated three times on the bottom two tiers and twice on the top two tiers, but feel free to do your own thing!). You will also need to go up over the top of the cake.

7 Cut out the leaves freehand (or using the templates provided if you are not confident) from the wafer paper. Stick them in place along the vines with the dimpled side facing out, using piping gel, as shown in the main photograph.

8 Use the piping bag filled with royal icing to pipe 'bumpy' stitched lines over the scored vines (see 'Bumpy' Piping). Pipe tiny leaves at the end of each vine **(D)**, outlining the shape first and filling in by zigzagging back and forth in-between the outline. Now outline the wafer paper leaves and flowers and pipe in the details **(E)**.

9 Pipe groups of three blossoms, evenly spaced along the horizontal sections of the trim, around the bottom tier. Squeeze out tiny teardrops and pull the piping tip into the centre for each petal **(F)**.

10 Punch out about 50 small blossoms from wafer paper using the blossom punch (see Wafer Paper Techniques) **(G)**. Stick them onto the cake using a little piping gel.

11 Mix some pearl lustre dust with clear alcohol or lemon extract and paint over all the royal iced lines (for the vines and outlines).

Tip

The piping doesn't need to be perfect. Try squeezing the royal icing out generously and dotting it along for a bumpy stitched effect.

C

D

E

F

G

Tip

Attach the wafer paper flowers with piping gel, as using edible glue can make the paper buckle. Hold the ends of the petals in place for a few seconds to make sure they are secure.

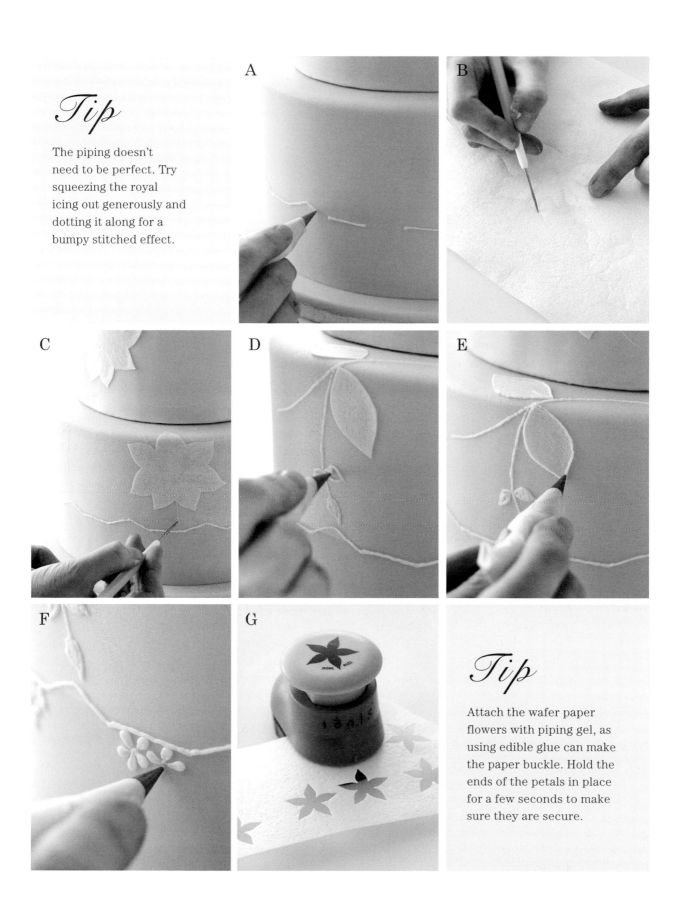

12 To make the lace flower appliqués thinly roll out the cream flower paste and dust the blossom mould with pearl lustre dust. Press the flower paste into the mould and dust again, and press the back of the mould on top. Carefully tear the excess paste away, then turn the icing lace out of the mould and set aside (see Using Moulds). Repeat to make another seven flowers.

13 Repeat Step 12 using the pale brown flower paste and the daisy mould.

14 Now repeat Step 12 using the white flower paste and the end section only of the floral V spray mould to make small blossoms **(H)**. Carefully cut around the flower and remove the excess paste.

15 Attach the appliqués onto the cake using edible glue. Stick some edible sequins – either made using the sequin mould and cake lace mix (see Edible Sequins) or shop-bought – into the centre of the larger appliqués with edible glue. Stick the tiny pearl dragees to the smaller blossoms.

16 Finish by securing satin ribbon around the base board (see Securing Ribbon Around Cakes and Boards). Make 'sludge' with the pale coffee-coloured sugarpaste and pipe between the tiers to fill in any gaps (see Piping with Sludge).

H

Couture Mini Cakes

These chic mini cakes are created using the same techniques as for the main cake. The caramel-coloured piped details and painted leaves look striking against the white sugarpaste covering and the floral appliqué details add a stylish element.

YOU'LL ALSO NEED

- Round mini cakes (see Mini Cakes) iced in white sugarpaste (rolled fondant)
- Caramel-coloured royal icing (see Royal Icing Recipe)
- Small piping (pastry) bag fitted with no.1 tube (tip)
- Brown food paste colouring
- Applique lace moulded flowers (see Steps 12–14 , Designed With Love)

Use caramel-coloured royal icing to freely pipe a nice curved vine up from the base of the cake at the front and back. You can come up over the top of the cake if you wish. Paint on the leaves freehand using brown food paste colouring and water instead of wafer paper. Pipe in the smaller leaf, flower and vine details in the same way as for the main cake (see Steps 8–9, Designed with Love). Add a couple of flower lace appliqués using edible glue.

Ornate Stencil Lace

Intricate lace decorations can be quite time-consuming, especially when they are completely customized to match a particular lace. However, like the many cake lace products now widely available, cake lace stencils are another way to create elaborately detailed lace effects quickly and easily. To give the cake design an extra dimension, I painted a lilac scalloped border on the base of the bottom tier and cake board, added piped details to the stencil patterns and brushed over all the royal icing with gold lustre dust for added shine.

YOU WILL NEED

MATERIALS

- 10cm (4in) square, 10cm (4in) deep; 15cm (6in) square, 11cm (4¼in) deep; 20cm (8in) square, 11.5cm (4½in) deep; and 28cm (11in) square, 11.5cm (4½in) deep cakes (see Cake Recipes), each iced in very pale dusky pink sugarpaste (rolled fondant) (see Covering with Sugarpaste)
- 35cm (14in) square cake board, iced in very pale dusky pink sugarpaste (see Icing Cake Boards)
- Edible dust: pink, purple and pearl white mixed with high alcohol content (95%+) clear alcohol; or lilac airbrush paint mixed from baby pink, purple and pearl
- Lustre dust: pearl; gold
- Royal icing (see Royal Icing Recipe): half quantity of caramel-coloured soft-peak (I use ivory/caramel Sugarflair paste colour); quarter quantity of uncoloured
- Paste or liquid food colouring: dusky pink to match the top three tiers (I used Sugarflair dusky pink/wine); dusky lilac for the bottom tier (I combined dusky pink with a little grape violet)
- Clear alcohol or lemon extract

EQUIPMENT

- Blossom spray and scallop border lace stencils by Zoë Clark (Designer Stencils)
- Scriber
- Dusting brushes: two large flat; one medium
- 16 hollow dowels cut to size of each tier (see Assembling Tiered Cakes)
- Masking tape
- Fine paintbrush
- Three small piping (pastry) bags
- Piping tubes (tips): one no. 1; two no. 1.5
- 1.4m (1½yd) length of 1.5cm (⅝in) pink satin ribbon

1 Place the scallop lace border stencil against one of the sides of the bottom tier and use the scriber to mark the scallop border onto the icing **(A)**. Repeat for each side of the cake.

2 Using either the edible dusts mixed with alcohol (until it is quite liquid) or the mixed airbrush paints, paint a thin layer of the lilac shade beneath the scalloped line using a large flat brush (see Painting). Paint all the way around the cake, making sure the brushstrokes go in the same horizontal direction **(B)**.

3 Paint around each side of the cake board, about 5cm (2in) in from the edge, using brushstrokes in one direction. Paint a second layer onto the cake and around the board, making sure that the paint has dried between coats. Then paint one more layer on both and set aside to dry.

4 Using another large dry flat dusting brush, dry dust with pearl lustre only over the painted area on the cake and board; this will help to blend in the colours and mellow out the streaks (see Dry Dusting and Lustring).

5 Dowel and assemble the cake, using seven dowels in the bottom tier, five in the 20cm (8in) tier and four in the 15cm (6in) tier (see Assembling Tiered Cakes).

6 Gently mix and soften the caramel-coloured royal icing in a small bowl. Place a damp piece of kitchen paper (paper towel) over the top to prevent the icing from drying out while you are completing the stencil work.

7 Place the scallop lace border stencil back against one of the sides of the bottom tier, making sure it is central (use a ruler if necessary). Mask off both ends of the stencil with masking tape, allowing the pattern to go at close to the edge as possible but making sure the icing can't escape underneath as the corners round off slightly. Holding the cake steady, quickly but carefully smear some of the caramel royal icing in a thin layer across the stencil using the palette knife **(C)** (see Using Stencils).

8 Fairly quickly work a damp, medium-sized dusting brush down the icing across the stencil to achieve a more stitch-like texture. You may need to clean and re-dampen your brush a couple of times during this process **(D)**.

9 Carefully peel off the stencil to reveal the pattern **(E)**. Then use a damp fine paintbrush to neaten up any stray pieces of icing, particularly at the ends. Repeat for each side of the cake, washing and drying the stencil thoroughly between uses.

10 To mark the flower design onto the bottom tier, first mask off the main flower and a couple of leaves on the smallest stencil **(F)**, making sure the icing previously stencilled is dry. Stencil the detail onto the cake using the main photograph as a guide, then use a medium flat brush to texture the icing, as in Step 8. To avoid smudging your work, stencil alternate flowers to allow them to dry before stencilling the flowers in-between. The flowers in the corners might not fit completely: you may need to stencil part of the flower only. Pat down or remove any smudged or excess icing with a damp fine paintbrush.

11 Stencil the top three tiers in the same way, using the medium-sized stencil for the 20cm (8in) tier and the smallest stencil for the 15cm (6in) tier. The motif on the top tier is made with the stencil used on the 20cm (8in) tier.

A

B

Tip

Less is more – try not to brush back and forth over the same area too much, as it can spoil the look.

C

D

E

Tip

You may be able to use the stencil multiple times, but as soon as it gets messy – particularly on the underside – make sure you wash it before stencilling again.

F

12 Fill the piping bag fitted with a no. 1 tube with soft-peak caramel-coloured royal icing and pipe small scallops around the bottom of the stenciled border (**G**). Now pipe in the additional lines on the rest of the cake using the main photograph as a guide – above the blossoms around the base of the scallop border and a tiny vine at the base of the motifs on the 20cm (8in) tier.

13 Pipe in the leaf details on all the tiers by piping a dot for the vines and pulling the icing outwards (**H**). Pipe dots for the flower centres (**I**). Make sure the corners are all finished neatly.

14 Fill a piping bag fitted with a no. 1.5 tube with 30ml (2 tbsp) of royal icing mixed with pale dusky pink food colouring to a soft-peak consistency. Pipe a snail trial border around the top three tiers (see Piping with Royal Icing) (**J**). Repeat around the bottom tier, this time using royal icing mixed with dusky lilac food colouring.

15 Mix some gold lustre dust with clear alcohol and paint over all the royal icing details (**K**). Finish by securing satin ribbon around the base board (see Attaching Ribbon Around Cakes and Boards).

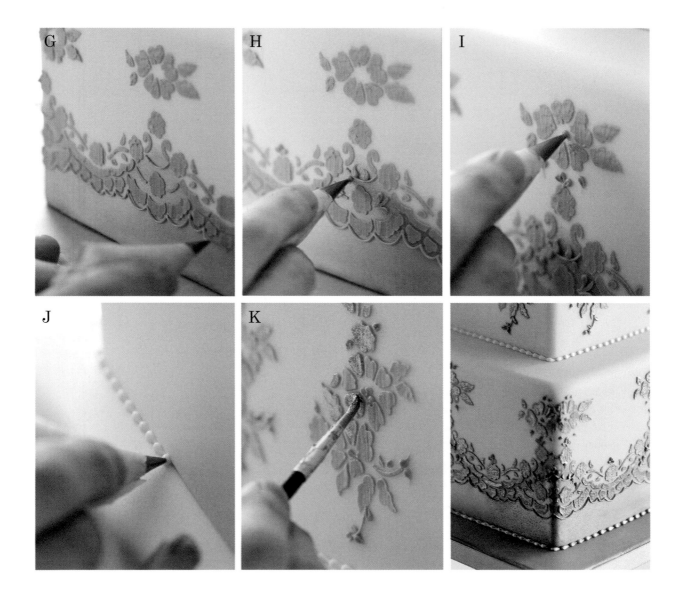

Floral Stencil Cookies

Stencilling is a quick and easy way to add intricate detail to cookies. The cookie bases can either be covered in sugarpaste or outlined and flooded with royal icing. Here I have worked a delicate floral design in pale lilac royal icing and added pearl dragées for a pretty finishing touch.

YOU'LL ALSO NEED

- 10cm (4in) oval cookies (see Baking Cookies) covered in pale dusky pink sugarpaste (rolled fondant) (see Covering Cookies with Sugarpaste) or outlined and flooded in royal icing (see Royal-Iced Cookies)
- Small or medium stencil with flower and leaf detail by Zoë Clark (Designer Stencils)
- Dusky lilac firm soft-peak royal icing (see Royal Icing Recipe)
- Tiny pearl dragées
- Pale lilac pearl lustre dust
- Clear alcohol

Cover parts of the stencil with masking tape to expose only the flower and leaf detail. Place the stencil over the centre of the cookie and work the design straight on top using a palette knife and the lilac royal icing (see Steps 6–7, Ornate Stencil Lace). Remove the stencil and use a damp fine paintbrush to brush down the design in a brush embroidery effect, removing any excess icing as you go (see Using Stencils).

Attach the dragées using tiny dots of royal icing or edible glue if covered with sugarpaste. Mix some of the pale lilac lustre dust with clear alcohol and paint over the stencilling detail.

Fancy Floral Embroidery

This beautiful three-tier square cake would make the perfect centrepiece for a wedding or silver anniversary party, and looks just as special as a single or two-tier design. The modern floral lace effect is made using zigzag embroidery. Quicker than traditional brush embroidery, this technique involves outlining the design then zigzagging back and forth between the lines. Use the templates to easily replicate the pattern or substitute these with your own unique designs. I enhanced the silver colour scheme by airbrushing beneath the pattern and brushing lustre dust over the piping to make it really stand out.

YOU WILL NEED

MATERIALS

- 10cm (4in) square, 10cm (4in) deep; 15cm (6in) square, 13cm (5in) deep; and 20cm (8in) square, 11.5cm (4½in) deep cakes (see Cake Recipes), each iced in white sugarpaste (rolled fondant) at least 24 hours in advance (see Covering with Sugarpaste)
- 25cm (10in) square cake drum iced in white sugarpaste at least 24 hours in advance (see Icing Cake Boards)
- Airbrush paint colours: silver or black mixed with white matt and pearl (or edible silver spray)
- Half quantity of royal icing (see Royal Icing Recipe)
- Black paste food colouring or gel
- Silver lustre dust
- Clear alcohol or lemon extract

EQUIPMENT

- Lace design templates (see Templates)
- Greaseproof paper (baking parchment) paper
- Pencil
- Pins
- Airbrush (optional)
- Small piping (pastry) bags
- No. 0 piping tube (tip)
- Cake scriber (optional)
- 8 hollow dowels cut to size of each tier (see Assembling Tiered Cakes)
- Fine paintbrush
- 1m (40in) length of 1.5cm (⅝in) white satin ribbon

1 Start by tracing your lace design onto the baking parchment. The templates provided (see Templates) have already been reversed for you – if you are using your own design, consider reversing it first. There are two designs per tier; one for the front and back and one for the two opposite sides.

2 Pin your patterns onto each side of all three tiers and transfer the markings onto the icing using a pencil (see Using Templates) **(A)**. You do not need to press very hard or follow the line continuously – I like to make little dashes. Once you have finished, carefully remove the pins and put them away. You should now be able to see the faint markings.

3 Place all three tiers onto greaseproof paper. Cut a strip or join two or three strips of greaseproof paper to fit around the base of the bottom tier. The strips should be 3.25cm (1½in) wide. Pin them to the cake, making sure they sit tightly up against the icing. Fill your airbrush with paint and lightly spray the bottom to give it a light silver tint (see Airbrushing and Spraying) **(B)**. If you don't have an airbrush, you can use silver edible spray.

4 Lightly spray the entire middle tier, aiming to achieve the same effect as the bottom tier. For the top tier, you will need to wrap 3.25cm (1½in) wide strips of greaseproof paper around the top of the cake and secure them in place with pins. Cover the top with a piece of kitchen paper (paper towel) or paper and pin in place, then airbrush around the bottom of the cake.

5 Colour the royal icing grey using black paste food colouring or gel to achieve a stiff, soft-peak consistency (see Royal Icing Recipe). Fill a piping bag fitted with a no. 0 piping tube with the coloured icing. Carefully and closely pipe on top of the lace design, making sure you are in a comfortable position and using your work surface to steady your hand **(C)**. Don't worry about starting and stopping or if the line is a little rough and bumpy – you are aiming for a stitched effect (see 'Bumpy' Piping). Once you have gone all the way around the tier, add in double lines here and there – this will add extra detail, replicating the stitching in the original piece of lace.

6 When you have finished outlining, fill in the flowers, leaves and vines by zigzagging back and forth between the piped lines **(D)**. Work as quickly as you like, but remember that it doesn't need to be perfect! Try to zigzag across the width of each petal and leaf, rather than vertically, as this will change the angles of your stitching as you work around each piece. Keep going until you have filled in the lace on all sides of each tier.

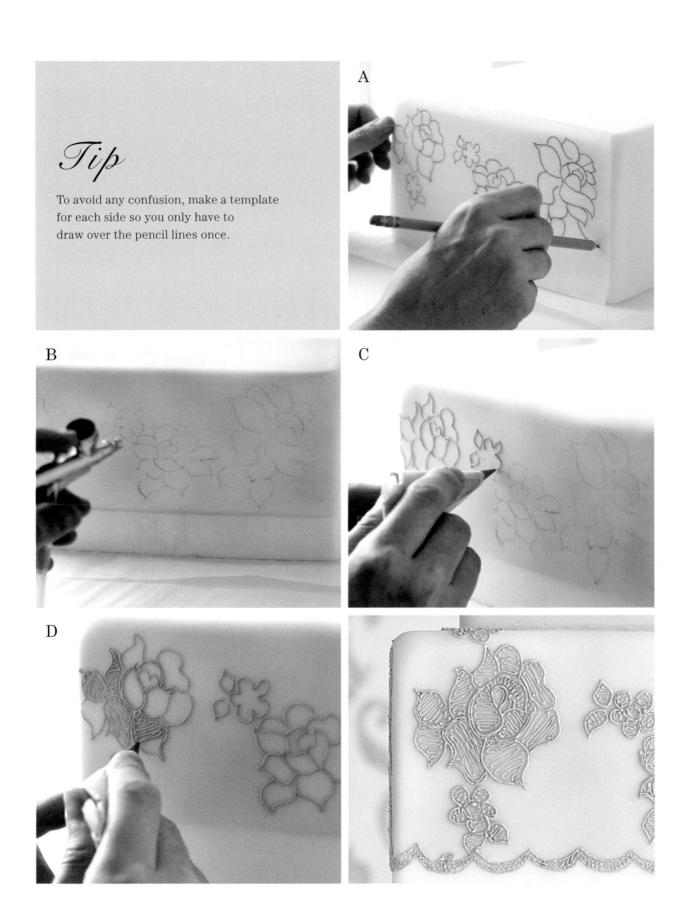

A

B

C

D

7 Next pipe the scallop border around the bottom tier. Mark indentations approximately 2cm (¾in) apart using a cake scriber or pin. Pipe a drop line scallop between each mark, working all the way around the cake. Next pipe a second line about 3–4mm (⅛in) underneath **(E)**. When you have finished, fill between the two lines with a small running zigzag 'stitch'. Change your piping bag if necessary and pipe the border in the same way on the top tier, this time with the scallops facing upwards. You will need to work closely to the cake, as you are going against gravity and don't want the lines to drop down.

8 Dowel the bottom and middle tiers and assemble the cake on the base board (see Assembling Tiered Cakes). Fill a piping bag with softened sugarpaste or royal icing and carefully fill in the gap between the tiers (see Piping with Sludge), or alternatively pipe a 'snail trail' border (see Piping with Royal Icing).

9 Mix some silver lustre dust with clear alcohol, or lemon extract, to a painting consistency and lightly brush over the piping **(F)**. Secure satin ribbon around the base board to finish (see Securing Ribbon Around Cakes and Boards).

E

F

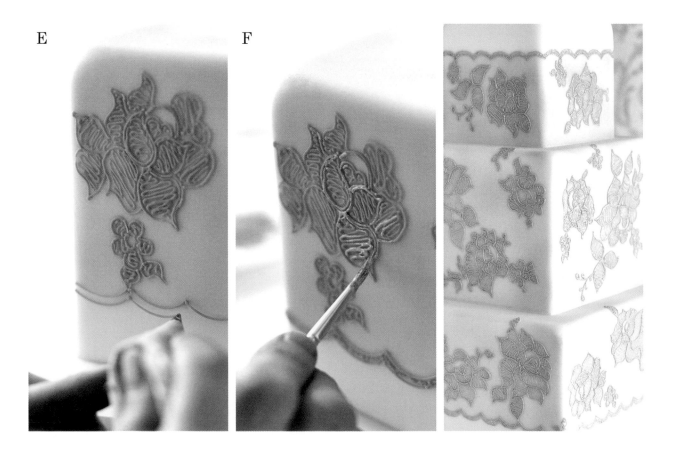

Embroidered Mini Cakes

These glamorous golden mini cakes are piped with the zigzag embroidery method using the same templates as for the tiered cake. Change the colour scheme to suit your theme or experiment by piping the design onto sugarpaste-covered cupcakes or cookies.

YOU'LL ALSO NEED

- Square mini cakes (see Mini Cakes) iced in white sugarpaste (rolled fondant)
- Fancy Floral Embroidery Lace design templates (see Templates)
- Airbrush filled with gold pearl airbrush paint (or use edible spray)
- Small piping (pastry) bag fitted with no. 0 tube (tip)
- Royal icing (see Royal Icing Recipe)
- Ivory paste food colouring
- Gold lustre dust
- Clear alcohol or lemon extract
- Gold satin ribbon

Trace small motifs or flowers from the templates onto baking parchment with a pencil and transfer the design onto the cakes (see Steps 1–2, Fancy Floral Embroidery). Use the airbrush or edible spray to lightly colour the icing.

Fill the piping bag with royal icing coloured with ivory food colouring. Pipe over the outlines and zigzag to fill in (see Steps 5–6, Fancy Floral Embroidery). When dry, mix the lustre with alcohol or lemon extract and lightly paint over the 'stitching'. Secure ribbon around the base of each cake to finish.

Little Blossom Laser Lace

While researching for this book I came across a lovely lace sharing my name – of course I had to include it! This particular "Zoë" style is known as laser lace: a fairly new design in dressmaking that features three-dimensional shapes, laser cut from satin and embroidered onto different fabrics to form striking patterns. I recreated the look by first cutting a pretty border of scallops, swirls and scrolls from flower paste, then embellishing the tiers with thin vines formed using a strip cutter, piped leaves and embroidery details. Finally, I added tiny wafer paper flowers to give the cake an elegant textured look.

YOU WILL NEED

MATERIALS

- 10cm (4in) square, 10cm (4in) deep; 15cm (6in) square, 11cm (4¼in) deep; and 20cm (8in) square, 11.5cm (4½in) deep cakes (see Cake Recipes), each iced in pale mint/eau de nil sugarpaste (rolled fondant) (see Covering with Sugarpaste)
- 28cm (11in) square cake drum iced in pale mint/eau de nil sugarpaste (see Icing Cake Boards)
- Half quantity of royal icing (see Royal Icing Recipe)
- Hot glue and glue gun (optional)
- 100g (3½oz) white flower (petal/gum) paste
- Two A4 sheets of wafer (rice) paper

EQUIPMENT

- Cake boards: two 18cm (7in) square; two 13cm (5in) square
- White satin ribbon: 3.5m (3¾yd) length of 2.5cm (1in); 115cm (1¼yd) length of 1.5cm (⅝in)
- 7.5cm (3in) square, 20cm (8in) deep cake dummy
- 7.5cm (3in) square, 5mm (¼in) thick piece of foam board
- Eight dowels cut to size of each tier (see Assembling Tiered Cakes)
- Broderie anglaise straight frill cutter (PME)
- Double scroll cutters (Stephen Benison)
- Cutting wheel
- Stitching tool
- Circle cutters: 3.75cm (1½in); 3cm (1¼in)
- 3mm (⅛in) strip cutter (no. 1 Jem)
- Small piping (pastry) bag with no. 1 piping tube (tip)
- Small flower paper punches: blossom; daisy; tiny daisy
- Flower cutters: small daisy; small primrose; small triple plunger blossom set (PME)
- Ball tool and foam pad

1 Stick the two 18cm (17in) boards together, wrap the 2.5cm (1in) wide ribbon around them twice to hide the join and secure with double-sided tape. Repeat for the two 13cm (5in) cake boards and set aside. Stick the 18cm (7in) boards to the centre of the 28cm (11in) iced base board using royal icing or hot glue(**A**). Stick the cake dummy onto the piece of foam board using royal icing or hot glue: this is used as a spacer to support the top tier, as these cake boards (13mm drums) are unavailable in smaller sizes.

2 Dowel the bottom and middle tiers using four dowels in each tier (see Assembling Tiered Cakes). You will need to ensure that the dowels will fit within the spacers that will be placed on top, rather than within the size of the tier above. Assemble the bottom tier on top of the 18cm (7in) double board, the middle tier on top of the 13cm (5in) double board and the top tier onto the cake dummy spacer. Secure everything in place with royal icing.

3 Start the decoration by thinly rolling out some white flower paste. Use the frill cutter to cut enough 5mm (¼in) wide parallel strips to go around each tier. You will need about 14 pieces cut from the length of the cutter (**B**). Carefully attach the strips to the base of each tier with a small amount of edible glue.

4 Roll out some more white flower paste and use the double scroll cutters to cut the decorative scrolls to go around the bottom of the tiers. Start with the top and bottom tiers and cut eight pieces from both parts of the set for the centre design on all sides of both tiers.

5 Use the cutting wheel to trim only the swirls from the shapes (**C**). Stick them onto the cakes using edible glue, with the larger swirls facing downwards and the smaller swirls facing upwards. Run the stitching tool through the centre of each piece – you could also do this before sticking the swirls onto the cake (**D**).

6 To make the central motif on the middle tier and the corners of the bottom tier, roll out some more flower paste and cut out four circles with the larger cutter, then take out the centres with the smaller circle cutter. Cut the shapes in half then cut the ends on an angle, as shown (**E**).

7 Cut out eight more scrolls from each cutter in the two-part set and use the cutting wheel to cut off the swirls. Run the stitching tool through the centre of each piece. Glue the half circles to the middle and bottom tiers, then attach the smaller swirls to the sides of the half circles (**F**). Stick eight of the larger swirls to the middle tier corners, trimming the adjoining pieces at an angle first if necessary so they sit nicely together

8 To make the embroidered vines, first roll out some flower paste and use the strip cutter to cut very narrow pieces about 15cm (6in) long (**G**). Attach them onto the cake with edible glue, cutting them to the desired length (**H**). There are two strips on each side of the top tier, two on each side of the middle tier and four on each side of the bottom tier. The pieces on the top tier run over the top edge to join in the middle, and the pieces on the middle and bottom tiers run over the top edge up to the spacers.

9 Fill the piping bag with soft-peak royal icing and pipe the rest of the vines on the cake (**I**), using the main photograph as a guide.

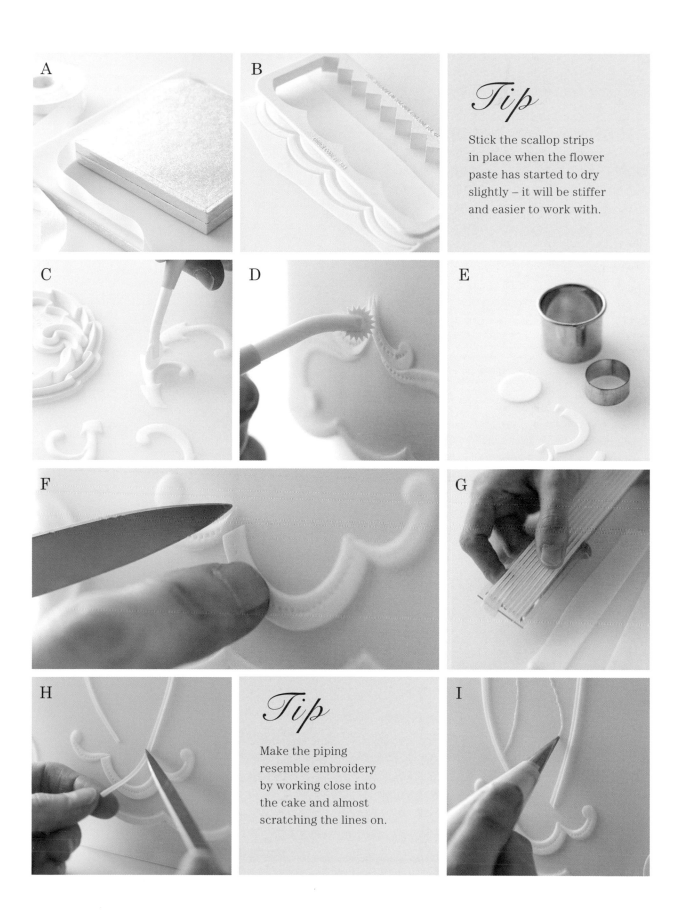

A

B

Tip

Stick the scallop strips in place when the flower paste has started to dry slightly – it will be stiffer and easier to work with.

C

D

E

F

G

H

Tip

Make the piping resemble embroidery by working close into the cake and almost scratching the lines on.

I

10 Pipe along the top edge of the scalloped trim a little at a time and brush down the icing with a damp brush **(J)** (see Brush Embroidery). Fill in any joins and gaps in the border as you go. Pipe tiny leaf outlines along the vines and brush in with a damp brush to fill them **(K)**.

11 Use the punches to cut 8 blossoms, 8 daisies and 80 tiny daisies from wafer paper **(L)**. Stick them onto the cake with a small amount of edible glue, taking care not to dissolve them. Reserve some of the tiny daisies for the centre of the primroses.

12 Thinly roll out more flower paste and use the cutters to make 16 primroses, 16 daisies, and the following from the plunger set: 16 large, 24 medium and about 100 small blossoms. Soften and cup the edges with a ball tool and foam pad before attaching the flowers to the cake with edible glue **(M)**. Attach the reserved daisies to the primrose centres. Secure the 1.5cm (⅝in) ribbon around the base board (see Securing Ribbon Around Cakes and Boards). Note: if you need to move the cake, leave the top tier off for transportation and stick it in place when you set the cake up. You will have to make the scallop trim around the bottom of the tier after it has been assembled.

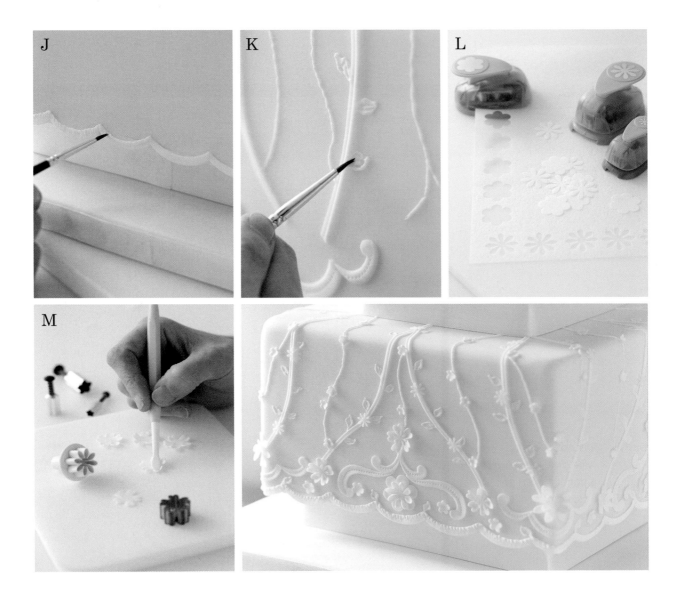

Blossom Laser Lace Cookies

These pretty heart-shaped cookies, embellished with a mixture of the techniques used to decorate the main cake, would make fabulous wedding favours. You can be really creative with your designs, selecting details that you like and adapting them to fit the cookie shape.

YOU'LL ALSO NEED

- Heart-shape cookies (see Baking Cookies) covered in pale mint/eau de nil sugarpaste (rolled fondant) (see Covering Cookies with Sugarpaste) or outlined and flooded in royal icing (see Royal-Iced Cookies)
- White flower (petal/gum) paste
- Cutters: Broderie anglaise straight frill (PME); small flower cutters
- Wafer (rice) paper
- Small flower punches
- 3mm ($\frac{1}{8}$) strip cutter (No. 1 Jem)
- Small piping (pastry) bag with no. 1 piping tube (tip) filled with soft-peak royal icing (see Royal Icing Recipe)

SCALLOP DETAIL COOKIES

Make the scallop design following Steps 3–7 of the main cake and varying the design to fit the cookie. Use the punches to cut out flowers of your choice from wafer paper, then make blossoms from flower paste using the cutters. Attach the flowers in place around the scallop design using edible glue.

FLORAL VINE COOKIES

Follow Step 8 from the main cake to cut out the vines from white flower paste. Use a piping bag filled with soft-peak royal icing to pipe the thinner vines and leaf details. Punch out small wafer paper flowers and use the cutters to cut small blossoms from flower paste, then attach in place on the vines using edible glue.

Lacy Appliqués and Leaves

As soon as I saw a picture of the stunning Oscar de la Renta dress that inspired this design, I knew straight away that it needed to be recreated in sugar. The sweet tumbling blossoms concentrated around the middle of the dress, the textured tulle netting backdrop and the matching scalloped veil translated beautifully onto this elegant four-tiered cake, with the help of lace mats, blossom cutters and a little piping work. I elevated the design onto two cake drums to allow for the graceful scallop drop.

YOU WILL NEED

MATERIALS

- 13cm (5in) round, 11.5cm (4½in) deep; 18cm (7in) round, 12cm (4¾in) deep; 23cm (9in) round, 13cm (5in) deep; and 28cm (11in) round, 13.5cm (5¼in) deep cakes (see Cake Recipes), each iced in ivory sugarpaste (rolled fondant) at least 24 hours in advance (see Covering with Sugarpaste)
- 38cm (15in) cake board iced in ivory sugarpaste at least 24 hours in advance (see Icing Cake Boards)
- Half quantity of royal icing (see Royal Icing Recipe)
- Clear alcohol
- Three quantities of original white cake lace mixes (Claire Bowman) (see Cake Lace)
- 100g (3½oz) white flower (petal/gum) paste
- Pearl lustre dust

EQUIPMENT

- Two 23cm (11in) cake drums
- Ivory satin ribbon: 1.8m (2yd) length of 2.5cm (1in); 1.25m (1¼yd) length of 1.5cm (⅝in)
- Leaves confectioners' mat (SugarVeil)
- Tiffany lace mat (Claire Bowman)
- 13 pieces of hollow dowel cut to size for each tier: 6 for the bottom tier; 4 for the 23cm (9in); 3 for the 18cm (7in) tier
- Five-petal blossom cutters: 2.7cm (1⅛in); 3.25 (1¼in); 4cm (1½in) (Orchard Products or PME)
- Multi-flower veiner mould (FMM)
- Circle cutters: 5mm (¼in); 7mm (⁵⁄₁₆in)
- Small piping (pastry) bag fitted with no. 1 piping tube (tip)

1 Stick the two 23cm (11in) cake drums together with royal icing and when they are dry, use more royal icing to stick them into the centre of the prepared iced cake board. Wrap some 2.5cm (1in) wide ivory satin ribbon twice around the drums (see Securing Ribbon Around Cakes and Boards) and secure with double–sided tape.

2 Make the cake lace in the leaves and Tiffany designs (see Cake Lace). You will need eight or nine full pieces of the leaves lace and three pieces of the Tiffany lace.

3 To cover the tiers in the leaves lace, first brush some clear alcohol onto the surface of the bottom tier, so that it is completely covered without being too wet. Use a piece of kitchen paper (paper towel) to pat it dry a little, if necessary: you want it to be tacky.

4 Trim the side of the lace using scissors so you have only the leaves design. Hold it up against the side of the bottom tier, so that the bottom of the lace is in front of the base of the cake. Carefully drape the lace over the icing, trying to avoid any creases: you should be able to peel back and reattach it if necessary **(A)**. Drape the lace over the top edge of the cake and trim away the folds and creases using scissors **(B)**.

5 Take a second piece of the leaves lace, trim as before and stick it onto the bottom tier, lining up the end neatly with the first piece to avoid any gaps. If the lace pieces overlap, they can be trimmed later. Attach and trim the lace over the top of the cake in the same way. Repeat the process once more to completely cover the cake, then trim the end where it meets the first piece. Set aside and repeat for the 23cm (9in) and 18cm (7in) tiers.

6 For the top tier, cut three rows of leaves to fit the height of the cake – the lace doesn't go over the top edge. Attach in the same way as in Steps 4–5 and trim to fit

using scissors. Don't worry if the lace doesn't match up perfectly, it won't be very noticeable.

7 Dowel and assemble the tiers onto the double-board base (see Assembling Tiered Cakes).

8 For the scallop bottom, trim away the bottom section of the Tiffany lace, so it is not as wide **(C)**. Attach the top lace section to the cake using edible glue, taking care not too use too much glue, to avoid dissolving the cake lace.

9 To make the flowers, thinly roll out some white flower paste and use the cutters to cut out blossoms of each size. Press each blossom into the multi-flower veiner mould, dusting the mould with pearl lustre dust each time **(D)** (see Using Moulds). Set the blossoms aside under a plastic sleeve until you have made a fair amount of all sizes: you will probably need about 200 blossoms in total, which can be made in two or three batches as you prefer.

10 To add a more lace-like, delicate feel, cut out the centre from each flower using the 5mm (¼in) circle cutter for the smaller blossoms and the 7mm (⁵⁄₁₆in) circle cutter for the other two sizes. Work on only a few blossoms of each size at a time and secure them onto the cake with edible glue. The petals will separate once the centre is cut, so stick the flowers back together on the cake, keeping a gap between the petals and a hole in the centre. Concentrate the flowers mainly around the 18cm (7in) tier and taper them towards the top and bottom of the cake, using the main photograph as a guide for placement.

11 Fill a piping bag fitted with no. 1 tube with soft-peak royal icing and pipe tiny dots for the centres of each flower **(E)**. Finish by securing the 1.5cm (⁵⁄₈in) ivory satin ribbon around the base board (see Securing Ribbon Around Cakes and Boards).

A

B

Tip

Don't worry if the cut edges of your lace don't match up: the pattern is so tight that it won't be too visible.

C

Tip

You can omit the central hole in the blossoms to save time: simply pipe the centres directly on top.

D

E

Garden Leaves Cake

This tall single-tiered cake makes a lovely garden party centrepiece. The fresh green leaves are made using the leaves confectioner's mat by SugarVeil, which gives them a realistic lacy vein texture. The moulded lace blossoms add a pretty finishing touch with their vibrant yellow centres.

YOU'LL ALSO NEED

- 18cm (7in), 15cm (6in) deep cake (see Cake Recipes), layered and filled with ganache (see Fillings and Coverings) and iced in ivory sugarpaste (rolled fondant) (see Covering with Sugarpaste)
- Green-coloured cake lace mix (I used mint green and gooseberry Sugarflair paste colours) and leaves confectioners' mat (SugarVeil) (see Cake Lace)
- Clear alcohol
- Flower (petal/gum) paste: white; yellow
- Pearl lustre dust
- Flower/leaves silicone lace mould (CK)

LEAVES

Cut out leaves of various sizes freehand from the leaves cake lace using scissors **(A)**. Use the central vein as a guide – it should run up the middle of each leaf. There will not be an outer border line, just the cut edge. Brush some clear alcohol onto the cake where the leaves are to be positioned and then attach the lace. Concentrate the leaves towards the top of the cake so they become sparser towards the base.

FLOWERS

Thinly roll out some white flower paste and dust the mould fairly well with pearl lustre dust (see Using Moulds). Press the paste into the mould to cover the flower entirely; it doesn't need to cover the leaves **(B)**. Dust over the back of the paste with more lustre and press the back of the mould on top. Carefully remove the paste and cut around the edge of the flower. Repeat to make 18 flowers and attach them randomly to the cake with edible glue.

To make the centres, roll petit pois-sized balls of yellow flower paste and press them into the flower centre of the mould **(C)**. Stick them in position on the flowers using edible glue.

A

B

C

Lace Ruffles and Ribbons

The 'Cake Lace Revolution' of recent years has made intricate and detailed lace cake designs easily achievable for cake decorators of all levels. Using lace mixes and mats, elaborate cake laces are so simple to make. The flexible nature of the lace means that it not only can be used to wrap around cakes, but it can also be ruffled and made into beautiful bows, as I've done here. I love the contrast between the soft pink and black layered ruffles on this striking tiered cake, perfect for celebrating with the girls.

YOU WILL NEED

MATERIALS

- 10cm (4in) round, 10cm (4in) deep; 15cm (6in) round, 11.5cm (4½in) deep; and 20cm (8in), 13cm (5in) deep cakes (see Cake Recipes), each iced in very pale pink sugarpaste (rolled fondant) (see Covering with Sugarpaste)
- 23cm (11in) cake board iced in black sugarpaste (see Icing Cake Boards)
- Cake lace mix (Claire Bowman or alternative): 3 x quantities of black to make 10 pieces of cake lace; 1 x quantity of very pale pink-coloured cake lace mix to make 3 pieces of cake lace (see Cake Lace)
- Clear alcohol (optional)
- Flower (petal/gum) paste: 150g (5½oz) very pale pink; 100g (3½oz) black

EQUIPMENT

- Pavoni (no. 4) cake lace mat
- Veining/frilling stick (Jem)
- 23cm (11in) length of 1.5cm (⅝in) black satin ribbon

1 Make the strips using the cake lace mixes and mats (see Cake Lace). Carefully cut one of the black lace strips in half down the centre using scissors **(A)**. Attach the pieces to the base of the middle tier with edible glue or by brushing a little water or clear alcohol onto the sugarpaste first, trim away the excess at the back.

2 Very thinly roll out strips of pale pink flower paste measuring approximately 30 × 6cm (12 × 2½in) – they need to be almost translucent. Trim to make them fairly even; they don't need perfectly straight and parallel edges. You will need about 11–12 strips for the ruffles on the bottom tier. Set them aside under a plastic sleeve to keep them fresh, while you work on a couple at a time.

3 Use the veining stick to thin, soften and ruffle along one side of three of the strips **(B)**. Brush a small amount of edible glue just up from the base around the bottom tier and attach the flower paste ruffles to the cake, folding in a slight pleating as you go **(C)**. Once you have attached one ruffle, stick the next one in place so that it overlaps slightly and they blend together neatly. Trim the ruffles once you have gone all the way around the cake and set any leftover paste aside under a plastic sleeve.

4 Brush some more edible glue onto the cake, about 2.5cm (1in) above the flower paste frills. Stick the cake lace pieces onto the cake: you will need about three cake lace strips to go once around the cake **(D)**. Trim away any excess, if necessary.

5 Repeat Steps 3 and 4 twice more, until you reach the top edge of the tier. For the ruffle over and around the top edge of the bottom tier, trim the width of the paste after frilling it so it fits neatly up against the base of the middle

tier. Pleat the flower paste off the cake first and check its size against the cake, then trim and stick it in position on the cake.

6 To make the bow around the top tier, start by rolling out three strips of black flower paste, each measuring 35 × 7cm (14 × 2¾in). Trim the strips neatly with a sharp knife, making sure the sides are parallel.

7 Use edible glue to carefully stick a piece of pale pink cake lace onto one of the black flower paste strips . Wrap it around the tier, securing it in place with more glue. Pinch the ends together to one side of the front of the cake base.

8 Cut 8cm (3¼in) pieces from one of the black flower paste strips and one of the pale pink cake lace pieces. Lightly stick them together and fold them in three lengthways to form the knot piece. Stick the remaining cake lace from the cut piece onto the trimmed flower paste strip and pinch the centre and two ends to form a bow, with the cake lace on the outside. Wrap the short piece around the centre of the bow, then secure with edible glue **(E)**.

9 Use the last pieces of black flower paste and pale pink cake lace for the tails. Pinch one end of each piece and cut the other end, at an angle, to your desired length **(F)**. Attach the two tails to the cake first, followed by the bow using edible glue. Pin in place carefully with a cocktail stick if necessary to support the weight until it is stuck well. Finish by securing satin ribbon around the base board (see Securing Ribbon Around Cakes and Boards).

A

B

C

Tip

You may need to add extra edible glue in places to help the lace to stick onto the cake.

D

E

F

Tip

Use some kitchen paper (paper towel) to help support the loops of the bow while they dry.

Ribbon Lace and Rosettes Cake

This two-tiered white iced cake is given bags of texture and style with its intricate cake lace covering and chic arrangement of rosettes and roses. The ribbon lace can be quite time-consuming to make at first, but with practise it becomes easier and the results are well worth the effort.

YOU'LL ALSO NEED

- 15cm (6in) round, 11cm (4¼in) deep; and 20cm (8in) round, 14cm (5½in) deep cakes (see Cake Recipes), both iced in white sugarpaste (rolled fondant) (see Covering with Sugarpaste)
- 25cm (10in) cake board iced in white sugarpaste (see Icing Cake Boards)
- Flower (petal/gum) paste: 50g (1¾oz) black; 150g (5½oz) white
- White cake lace mix (Claire Bowman or alternative) used with the 'Rose Mantilla' confectioners' mat (SugarVeil) to make three pieces of cake lace (see Cake Lace)
- Clear alcohol
- 2.3cm (⅞in) strip cutter (No. 4 Jem)
- Stitching tool
- Ball tool and foam pad
- Royal icing (see Royal Icing)
- 1m (40in) length of 1.5cm (⅝in) white satin ribbon

ROSETTES

Roll out the black flower paste and cut a 40 × 5cm (16 × 2in) strip. Then cut a similar-sized strip from cake lace, trimming the edges first. Lightly brush edible glue onto the lace to stick it to the flower paste. Roll up the paste like a ribbon rose, scrunching and pleating it as you go **(A)**. Squeeze the paste at the base and trim off any excess. Repeat to make two more rosettes and set aside to dry.

CAKE LACE

To decorate the bottom tier, first trim the ends of the white cake lace. Brush the cake with clear alcohol and stick the lace in place: you will need two pieces to cover the tiers. Trim the lace neatly at the back using scissors.

RIBBON LACE

Thinly roll out pieces of white flower paste to at least 38cm (15in) long. Use the strip cutter to cut 2.3cm (⅞in) wide strips, at least twice the length of the cutter, then cut each strip in half down the middle. Place the strips under a plastic sleeve while you work on each piece.

Take one strip and soften both sides using a ball tool on a foam pad **(B)**, then run the stitching tool down the centre. Tease and fold the strip in half lengthways and roll it up (using the end of a paintbrush to help you): tightly at the beginning and getting looser as you go. Leave a 3cm (1⅛in) length at the end, leading to the next rose. Set each rose aside to dry slightly while you work on the next.

Work on six to eight roses at a time before sticking them onto the cake with edible glue; they need to be fairly stiff but flexible enough to hold their shape when attached. You will need 36 roses to cover the sides of the 20cm (8in) tier.

Make six more roses for the top of the tier and let them dry a little before cutting them in half. The pieces will separate, but stick the half rosettes back together on the cake as you go so they sit neatly around the base of the top tier.

FINISHING TOUCHES

Attach the black rosettes onto the top tier with royal icing and secure satin ribbon around the base board (see Securing Ribbon Around Cakes and Boards).

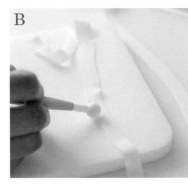

Contemporary Corded Lace

One of the most common types of lace we see on wedding dresses today is known as corded lace or Alençon lace; made by outlining lace details using a heaver or lustrous cording. Brides often send me lace swatches to replicate on their wedding cake and if the material is clean and of a good size I can emboss the design straight onto the icing, as I have done with the Elegant Embossed Cupcakes. Alternatively, the design can be traced onto baking (parchment) paper for use with the pencil transfer method, or piped onto plastic for embossing, as I have done for this cake.

YOU WILL NEED

MATERIALS

- 15cm (6in) round, 13cm (5in) deep; and 20cm (8in) round, 15cm (6in) deep cakes (see Cake Recipes), layered, filled and coated in buttercream or ganache (see Fillings and Coverings) and chilled
- 28cm (11in) cake board iced in white sugarpaste (rolled fondant) at least 24 hours in advance (see Icing Cake Boards)
- Quarter quantity of soft-peak royal icing (see Royal Icing Recipe)
- 1.25kg (2lb 12oz) white sugarpaste
- Pearl airbrush paint or lustre spray
- Pearl lustre dust
- Clear alcohol or lemon extract
- Sheet of A4 wafer (rice) paper

EQUIPMENT

- Templates: cord lace design; petal (see Templates)
- Pieces of rigid, strong plastic: 15 × 26cm (6 × 10¼in); 10 × 15cm (4 × 6in)
- Three small piping (pastry) bags
- Piping tubes (tips): nos. 1; 1.5; 0
- Dresden tool
- Airbrush or spray can
- Fine paintbrush
- Three hollow dowels cut to size of 20cm (8in) tier (see Assembling Tiered Cakes)
- Travel steamer or kettle
- 112cm (44in) length of 1.5cm (5/8in) white satin ribbon

1 At least an hour in advance and using the cord lace design template provided (see Templates) or your own pattern, pipe the design for the bottom tier onto the larger piece of rigid plastic with soft-peak royal icing and a piping bag fitted with a no.1 piping tube (A) (see Using Templates). Set it aside to dry.

2 Cover the 20cm (8in) cake in white sugarpaste (see Covering with Sugarpaste). Use the sharper end of a Dresden tool to score pleats into the icing on the front of the cake, starting from the top left edge and sweeping across to the bottom right to give an appearance of gathered dress fabric (B). Most pleats should sweep across the front, but you can also score a few that go straight down and to the back of the cake.

3 Carefully press the custom-made cord lace embossed design against the cake so the pattern goes over the scored lines (C). Ideally set the cake aside for a few hours or overnight to allow the icing to dry, making it easier to pipe on.

4 Clean the plastic, or use the smaller piece, and pipe on the top tier design as in Step 1. Set aside so the piping dries completely.

5 Cover the 15cm (6in) tier with white sugarpaste and score pleats with the Dresden tool, this time sweeping from the bottom left corner up and across to the right.

Press the new embossed design into the paste to mark on the lace pattern and set the cake aside for up to 24 hours to allow the sugarpaste to harden. Note: if you are using the pencil transfer method (see Using Templates) you will need to score the pleats while the icing is soft and wait at least 24 hours before transferring the design onto the cake.

6 Spray the tiers and base board separately with pearl airbrush paint or lustre spray, either using an airbrush or a spray can.

7 Place some soft-peak royal icing in a piping bag fitted with no. 1.5 tube and carefully fill in the scored grooves that fall inside the floral lace design. Use your finger to smooth the icing over the ridges. If the gaps aren't filled in advance you will see ridges in the pattern after working the brush embroidery. Repeat for both tiers.

8 For the brush embroidery, start by piping a small section of the pattern outline (D). Work on a little of the pattern at a time – if you pipe out too much, the icing can dry out before you brush it down and it will need to be redone. With a damp paintbrush, pat or 'brush' down the outline, from the outside of the pattern towards the inside, working along the freshly piped line (E) (see Brush Embroidery). Once you have finished the section you are working on, move along and pipe another section. Repeat the process around the entire pattern on both tiers.

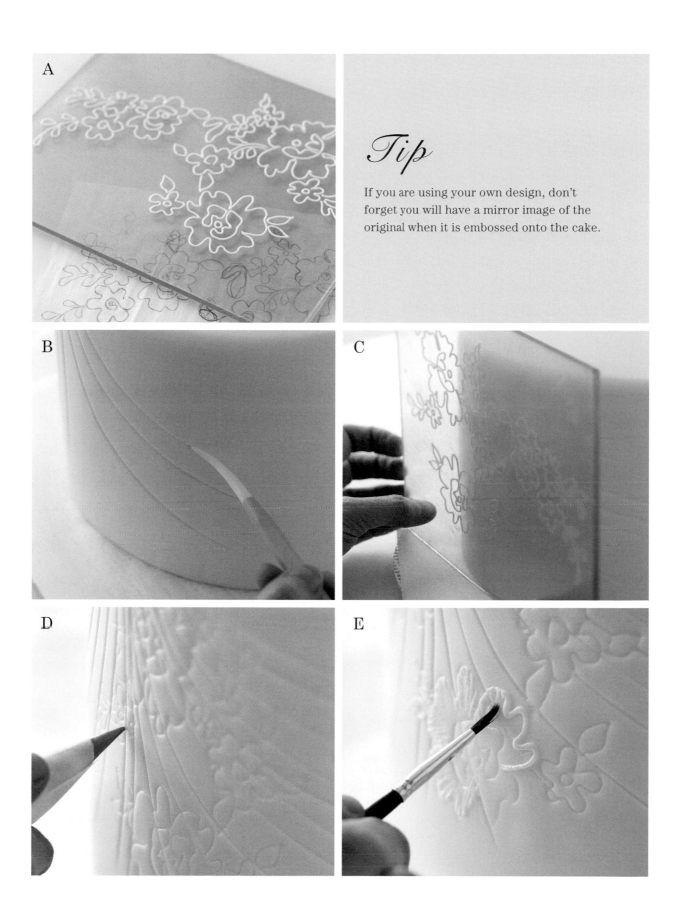

A

Tip

If you are using your own design, don't forget you will have a mirror image of the original when it is embossed onto the cake.

B

C

D

E

9 Dowel and assemble the tiers on the base board (see Assembling Tiered Cakes).

10 Mix some of the clear alcohol or lemon extract with some pearl lustre dust and paint over the brushwork **(F)**.

11 Place some more soft-peak royal icing into a piping bag fitted with no. 0 tip and carefully pipe around the outline of the design **(G)**. The piping doesn't have to be perfect, but you need to stay close to the cake with the piping tip, so the icing attaches securely without falling away with gravity. Use a damp paintbrush where necessary to dab down any stray pieces.

12 To make the flower, first cut out an 18cm (7in) diameter circle and five petals from wafer paper using the petal template provided (see Templates).

13 Cut a spiral into the circle and remove the inner circle using scissors **(H)**.

14 Apply a little edible glue around the inside cut line of the spiral, taking care not to use too much, as the wafer paper could dissolve. Starting from the outside, roll the end of the spiral inwards to form a quilled paper

rose **(I)**. As you are rolling, make sure the base of the flower is always sitting flat, ideally on your thumb, rather than concentrating on the alignment of the top – the rose should naturally open slightly towards the end **(J)**. If necessary, add more glue as you go.

15 Cut small slits in the base of each petal **(K)**. Brush a small amount of edible glue onto one side of the slit at the base of each petal. Stick the other side of the slit on top so it overlaps, making the petal cup inwards. Use a travel steamer or kettle to carefully steam the petals, one at a time, to soften and shape the paper **(L)**. Tease each petal with your fingers to give them a natural appearance, similar to a rose petal.

16 Glue the base of the petals once again and stick them to the base of the flower centre in a spiral **(M)**. If you can't manage to tuck the last petal inside the first, just let it overlap on both sides **(N)**.

17 Stick the flower onto the cake with royal icing. If you have a large gap between the petals, cut and shape a sixth petal to tuck in. Finish by securing satin ribbon around the base board (see Securing Ribbon Around Cakes and Boards).

F

G

Tip

Don't worry if your piping is slightly bumpy – it is supposed to look like stitching.

H

I

J

K

Tip

Make a few flowers if you are a beginner to help you to get into the swing of it!

L

M

N

Elegant Embossed Cupcakes

These stunning silver cupcakes can be made either simply by pressing a piece of corded lace directly into the design or by using a piped embosser to transfer the pattern. Brush embroider and outline the pattern as for the main cake for a delicately detailed effect.

YOU'LL ALSO NEED

- Cupcakes (see Baking Cupcakes) in silver foil cupcake cases (liners), freshly covered with grey sugarpaste (rolled fondant) (see Covering Cupcakes with Sugarpaste)
- Piece of cord lace or custom-made embosser
- Pearl lustre dust
- Clear alcohol or lemon extract
- Soft-peak royal icing (see Royal Icing Recipe)
- Two piping (pastry) bags
- Piping tubes (tips): no.s 1.5 and 0

Press your piece of cord lace (**A**) or custom-made embosser (see Step 1, Contemporary Corded Lace) into the soft sugarpaste to mark the pattern onto the cupcake (**B**).

Mix some pearl lustre with clear alcohol or lemon extract so it is quite liquid and paint it over the sugarpaste covering, using even brushstrokes in one direction. Try not to make the cupcake too wet. Leave to dry for about five minutes and then repeat to build up the pearlized effect. Repeat once again if necessary.

Brush embroider and outline the design (see Steps 8 and 11, Contemporary Corded Lace) using soft-peak royal icing and the piping bags fitted with a no. 1.5 tube for piping and a no. 0 tube for outlining.

A

B

Gorgeous Guipure Lace

Guipure or Venetian lace is one of the prettiest and oldest types of lace. Made up of a repeating motif, usually in a floral or geometric pattern, it is typically more textured than other laces and is connected by short embroidered stitches. I have recreated this effect by texturing flower paste floral appliqués with lace moulds: some using the whole part of the mould and some using only parts. I must confess, I've probably gone a little overboard with the amount of cutters and moulds used here, but you can easily cut back and use even half as many to achieve a really good result.

YOU WILL NEED

MATERIALS

- 10cm (4in) round, 10cm (4in) deep; and 28cm (11in) octagonal, 13.5cm (5¼in) deep cakes (see Cake Recipes), both iced in nude-coloured sugarpaste (rolled fondant) (see Covering with Sugarpaste) and sprayed with champagne-pink pearl airbrush paint (or lightly sprayed with pearl edible spray) (see Airbrushing and Spraying)
- 15cm (6in) round, 13cm (5in) deep; and 20cm (8in) round, 7.5cm (3in) deep cakes, both iced in pale ivory sugarpaste and sprayed in pearl white lustre/paint
- One 35cm (14in) cake board iced in pale ivory sugarpaste (see Icing Cake Boards)
- 200g (7oz) white flower (petal/gum) paste
- Edible white dust
- Half quantity of royal icing (see Royal Icing Recipe)

EQUIPMENT

- 12 pieces hollow dowel cut to size of each tier (see Assembling Tiered Cakes)
- Flower cutters: second largest cutter from lace flower cutter set (Orchard Products); 4.5cm (1¾in) eight-petal pointed daisy; 4cm (1½in) eight-petal rounded daisy; 4cm (1½in) six-petal pointed daisy; 3.25cm (1¼in) six-petal rounded daisy; 3.25cm (1¼in) stephanotis; 2cm (¾in) stephanotis; 2cm (¾in) primrose; small blossom cutter (largest from PME blossom/forget-me-not metal plunger cutters)
- Silicone appliqué lace moulds: 7.5cm (3in) flower spray; flowers (1482); flower designs (1601); 11.5cm (4½in) flowers (1026) (CK); mini daisy single (Decorate the Cake)
- Circle cutters: 1cm (³⁄₈in); 1.5cm (⁵⁄₈in)
- Small piping (pastry) bag fitted with no.1 piping tube (tip)
- Cream satin ribbon: 1.5m (1⅝yd) length of 5cm (2in) wide for the bow; 1.4m (1½yd) length of 1.5cm (⅝in) for the board

1 Start by dowelling and assembling the tiers onto the base board (see Assembling Tiered Cakes). Make some white and nude coloured 'sludge' and pipe around the base of the tiers to fill any gaps (see Piping with Sludge).

2 Thinly roll out some white flower paste and cut out about 19–20 of the largest flowers using the lace flower cutter.

3 Heavily brush the flower spray mould with white dust and press in the flowers to texture them with a lace pattern (see Using Moulds) (A). There is no need to match up the two pieces of the mould. Stick the flowers onto the cake in a random pattern, spacing them fairly evenly apart.

4 The pattern comes down to the top edge of the bottom tier and slightly down the corners. Place four large flowers randomly around the top of the bottom tier, leaving a gap between each one (see Appliqués). You don't need to place them in the same position on each corner.

5 Next, roll out some more flower paste and cut out about 30 pointed and 30 rounded eight-petal daisies. Press each one into the centre of the flower on the flower mould (1482) to add texture to them, dusting the mould with edible white dust with each use (B).

6 Cut out the centre of the pointed daisies with the 1cm (⅜in) circle cutter (C). Stick them onto the cake randomly, but spaced fairly evenly apart.

7 Next, cut out the six-petal pointed daisies and press them into the daisy lace mould, dusting as before. You will need about 25–30 daisies (D). Attach them onto the cake in and amongst the rest of the flowers. As the pattern becomes denser, stick some of the appliqués quite close together, or even touching each other.

8 Roll out some more flower paste and cut out 30 each of the larger stephanotis and the rounded six-petal daisies. Press them individually into the flower spray mould, as in Step 3 (E).

9 Make some small blossoms by using the two blossom sections of the flower designs mould and the centre flower from the 11.5cm (4½in) flower mould (F). You will need ten of each design. Stick them onto the cake, spacing them evenly apart.

10 Cut out about 20 each of the small primroses, small stephanotis, small plunger blossoms and 1cm (⅜in) and 1.5cm (⅝in) circles. Dust the 11.5cm (4½in) flower mould and press the shapes in to give them a nice texture with a pattern that stems from the middle, like the centre of a flower (G).

11 Stick the smaller flowers and circles to the cake, filling in all the gaps. You may not need all of them, or you may need to cut a few more.

12 When the cake is covered sufficiently, fill the piping bag with soft-peak royal icing and pipe dots around the circle appliqués and in the cut out holes in the flowers.

13 Pipe tiny connecting lines between each flower, using the main photograph as a guide (see Traditional Piping). As a general rule, connect up the shortest distances between the shapes (H). Use a damp paintbrush to pat down the icing at the ends of the lines to connect the piped embroidery lines with the lace appliqués.

14 Secure the 1.5cm (⅝in) wide satin ribbon around the base board (see Securing Ribbon Around Cakes and Boards). To finish, wrap the 50cm (20in) wide ribbon around the middle tier and tie it in a pretty bow.

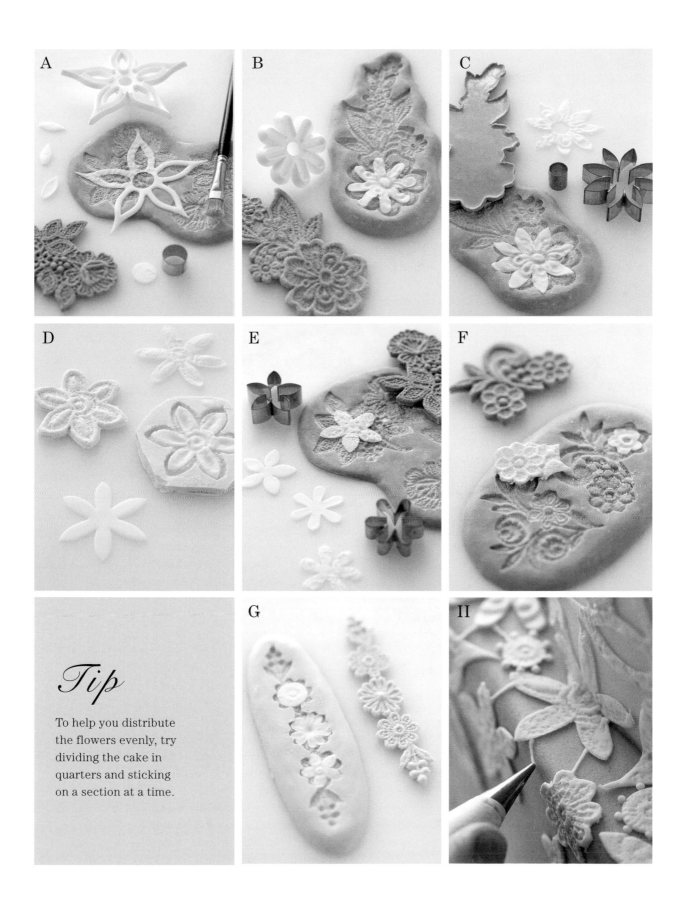

A

B

C

D

E

F

Tip

To help you distribute
the flowers evenly, try
dividing the cake in
quarters and sticking
on a section at a time.

G

H

Striking Circles Cake

This bold and beautiful cake gives Guipure lace a modern twist with its monochrome colour scheme. Cut the discs from textured black flower paste using a range of circle cutters and add connecting piping details for an eye-catching effect.

YOU'LL ALSO NEED
- 15cm (6in) round, 11.5cm (4½in) deep cake (see Cake Recipes), iced in white sugarpaste (rolled fondant) (see Covering with Sugarpaste)
- 100g (3½oz) black flower (petal/gum) paste
- Flower spray mould (CK) or similar
- Circle cutters: 4.5cm (1¾in); 3.75cm (1½in); 3cm (1¼in); 2.25cm (⅞in); 1.5cm (⅝in); 1cm (³⁄₈in)
- No. 7 piping tube (tip)
- Small piping (pastry) bag fitted with no. 1 piping tube filled with soft-peak black royal icing (see Royal Icing Recipe)

WHEELS
Thinly roll out the black flower paste and texture it using the flower spray mould (see Step 3, Gorgeous Guipure Lace). Cut out 12 circles using the largest cutter, and from these cut out 3.75cm (1½in) circles. Glue the 'wheels' around the top and bottom edges, so the bottom circles are positioned in the spaces between the top ones. Leave a 5cm (2in) border between the circles and the top and bottom of the cake.

Cut out more 'wheels' from leftover paste using the 3cm (1¼in) cutter for the outer edge and the 2.25cm (⅞in) cutter for the inside. Glue them onto the cake, weaving through the spaces between the larger circles. Keep the discs under a plastic sleeve to prevent them from drying out while you work.

Cut 1.5cm (⅝in) circles from leftover 2.25cm (⅞in) discs and secure them onto the cake between the larger circles. Now cut 1cm (³⁄₈in) circles from leftover 1.5cm (⅝in) discs and stick them into the centre of the largest wheels.

Use the no. 7 piping tube to cut out the centres from leftover 1cm (³⁄₈in) discs and stick them into the centres of the medium-sized wheels. Stick the leftover no. 7 tube cut-outs into the centres of the smallest wheels.

PIPING
Pipe all the connecting lines within and between the wheels, using the photograph as a guide. Use a damp paintbrush to pat down any stray ends so the lace looks neatly connected.

Royal-Iced Butterfly Garden

This gorgeous garden-themed cake gives a modern feel to the traditional royal-iced lace piping technique. The butterflies, daisies and garden fence border details are intricately piped from the templates provided using more advanced classic royal icing techniques, and are carefully secured onto the cake. This delicate work requires a very steady hand, as the decorations are extremely fragile however, the finished result is worthwhile. If you find the piping methods too fiddly and frustrating or are short of time, try using cake lace instead, as I have done with the Cake Lace Cupcakes, or a combination of both. The royal-iced decorations need plenty of drying time so it's a good idea to start them a couple of days in advance.

YOU WILL NEED

MATERIALS

- 15cm (6in) round, 11.5cm (4½in) deep; and 20cm (8in) round, 15cm (6in) deep cakes (see Cake Recipes), both iced in pale blue (Sugarflair Baby Blue) sugarpaste (rolled fondant) (see Covering with Sugarpaste)
- 28cm (11in) cake board, iced in pale green (Sugarflair Mint and Gooseberry) sugarpaste (see Icing Cake Boards)
- Half quantity of royal icing (see Royal Icing Recipe)
- Paste or liquid food colouring: yellow; baby blue; green (to match the sugarpaste)

EQUIPMENT

- Three dowels cut to size of 20cm (8in) tier (see Assembling Tiered Cakes)
- Three small piping (pastry) bags
- Piping tubes (tips): no.s 0; 1; 1.5
- Templates: butterflies; daisy petal; small flowers; garden fence lace border (see Templates)
- Four A4 plastic sleeves (or thin acetate) with flat boards or books
- Concertina card lined with baking (parchment) paper or greaseproof paper
- 112cm (44in) length of 1.5cm (⅝in) white satin ribbon

1 Dowel and assemble the cakes (see Assembling Tiered Cakes).

2 Start by making the butterflies (see Traditional Piping). Fill a piping bag fitted with a no. 1 tip with soft-peak royal icing. Cover the butterfly templates (see Templates) with a plastic sleeve and place on top of a board or book. Carefully pipe the outline of the butterfly: you will need three butterflies of each design (A). Next fill in the main structural elements of the wings – these are the slightly thicker lines on the template (B). Repeat for each butterfly.

3 Fill a piping bag fitted with a no. 0 tip with soft-peak royal icing and pipe in the finer details. For the lattice work, pipe all the vertical lines first and allow the icing to dry to avoid breakages (C). Use a damp brush to pat down any stray ends (D) and once dry, pipe on the horizontal lines (E). Set the butterflies aside to dry for at least six to eight hours, or overnight.

4 Cut one of the plastic sleeves in half, then cut one half into 6 x 2cm (1½ x ¾in) pieces. You will need 32 pieces, plus a few extra for any breakages. To make the main daisy, fill a piping bag fitted with a no. 1 tip with soft-peak royal icing and place one of the plastic pieces over the petal template. Stick it onto the paper using a small amount of royal icing to prevent it from moving

about. Now pipe the outline of the petal and the two vertical lines within and set them aside to dry overnight in a slightly curved position, such as in a shallow plate.

5 Once dry, pipe tiny lines down each side of the petal using a piping bag fitted with a no. 1 piping tube filled with fresh royal icing (F). When these are dry (after about 20 minutes), carefully peel the plastic from the petals. Assemble four petals for each flower onto a fresh square piece of plastic sleeve and use royal icing to hold them together in the centre (G).

6 Next stick another four petals in-between the petals of the first layer. Use kitchen paper (paper towel) or slightly curled up pieces of acetate or plastic around the outside of the flower, so that it dries in a slightly curved shape (H).

7 Once dry, mix some yellow food colouring into some soft-peak royal icing and pipe a collection of dots into the centre of each daisy (I). Set the daisies aside to dry completely (ideally overnight).

8 To make the small flowers, pipe the outlines and dotted centres over the template in the same way, using a small piping bag filled with royal icing and a no. 1 piping tube. You will need at least twelve flowers: vary the template design freehand for six flowers. Set aside to dry.

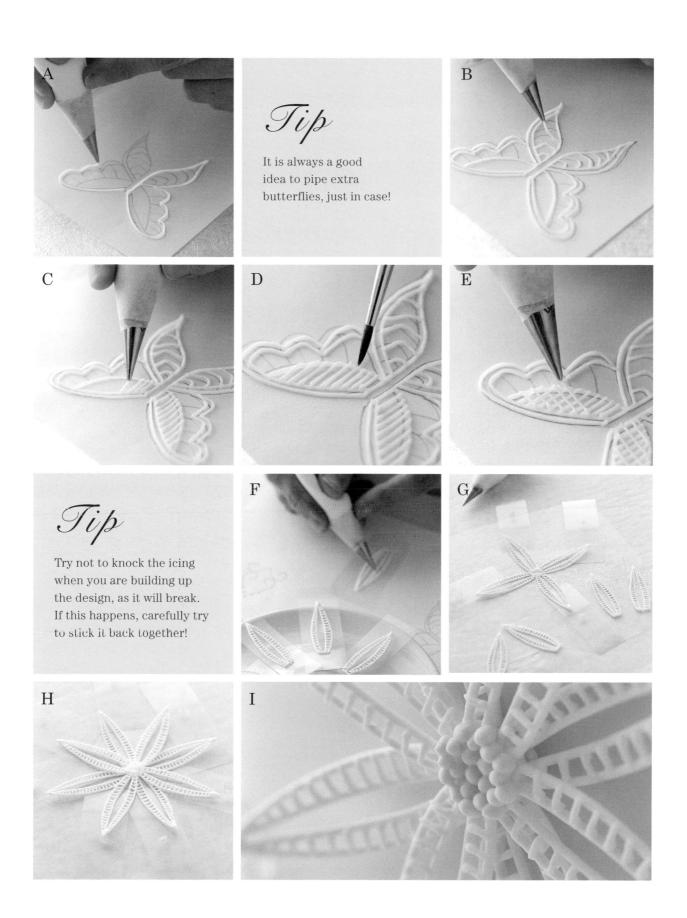

A

B

C

D

E

F

G

H

I

Tip

It is always a good idea to pipe extra butterflies, just in case!

Tip

Try not to knock the icing when you are building up the design, as it will break. If this happens, carefully try to stick it back together!

9 Make the little garden fence lace border pieces around the base of the cake in the same way using a no. 1.5 piping tube on a plastic sleeve or acetate, using the template provided (see Templates). Pipe the heart shape first for each one, then the swirl and finally the dots. You will need around 30 pieces: make sure you leave enough space on the plastic sleeve or acetate between each one and set aside to dry.

10 To assemble the butterflies, carefully remove the plastic to release the wings, peeling downwards and using the edge of the work surface to help you (**J**). Work on one piece at a time and set the pieces aside when released.

11 Place the concertina card lined with paper on a tray (so you can move it around) and fill a fresh piping bag fitted with a no. 1 or no. 1.5 tube with royal icing. Pipe a small amount of icing into the crease of the greaseproof paper and attach the wings (**K**). Pipe a dot for the head and a teardrop for the body (**L**). Set the butterflies aside to dry for at least a few hours, or overnight.

12 Use a small piping bag fitted with a no. 1.5 tube filled with soft-peak royal icing mixed with baby blue food colouring to pipe a snail trail (see Piping with Royal Icing) around the base of the top tier. Repeat with pale green icing around the base of the bottom tier. Colour enough green royal icing to fill another piping bag fitted with a no. 1 tube.

13 Tilt the cake very slightly, placing a board or book underneath. Using the piping bag fitted with the 1.5 tip filled with pale green royal icing, carefully pipe slightly curved lines down the side of the cake. Start with the main daisy stems, which are made from double lines between 10–12cm (4–4¾in) long (**M**). Then pipe slightly shorter single stems for the smaller flowers between the daisies. Keep in mind where the flower heads will be positioned on the cake to ensure you leave enough space between the stems and keep the lines as neat as possible. Use the green royal icing in the piping bag with a no. 1 tube to carefully pipe dots down the daisy stems (**N**).

14 Now for the scary part! Very carefully remove the butterflies from the cardboard and stick them onto the cake using a piping bag (without a tube) filled with fairly stiff-peak royal icing and a steady hand! You may need to hold the butterflies in place for ten seconds or so until they adhere. Use the main photograph as a guide for positioning the butterflies; it is best to decorate the top tier first to avoid knocking any decorations on the bottom tier (**O**). Next, use the stiff royal icing to stick on the daisies followed by the smaller flowers and any other butterflies onto the bottom tier.

15 Stick the garden fence lace border pieces around the cake, securing each piece one at a time onto the base board, about 1cm (⅜in) away from the cake. To do this, squeeze a tiny dot of royal icing onto the bottom middle point of each piece (**P**). Carefully stick it down and hold it in position for 30 seconds or so to adhere (**Q**), then move on to the next piece. Work all the way around the cake: if you have a gap at the end, try to disguise it by spacing the last few pieces further apart – this can be the back of the cake! Finish by securing satin ribbon around the base board (see Securing Ribbon Around Cakes and Boards).

J

K

L

M

N

O

P

Q

Tip

Warning: the piped butterflies are extremely fragile. Handle with care!

Tip

Lift the icing out and away from the cake slightly as you pipe to allow it to flow smoothly – if you work too close in, the icing will be little bumpy.

Cake Lace Cupcakes

These charming cupcakes continue the theme of the main cake without the time-consuming, intricate piping work. The butterflies and flowers are quick to make using a cake lace mix and mats and are simply glued onto the cupcakes for a pretty effect.

YOU'LL ALSO NEED

- Cupcakes (see Baking Cupcakes) in silver foil cupcake cases (liners), freshly covered with pale blue sugarpaste (rolled fondant) (see Covering Cupcakes with Sugarpaste)
- Small tub of pearl cake lace mix (Claire Bowman or alternative) (see Cake Lace)
- Lace mats: Butterflies (Claire Bowman); Isis (Crystal Candy, or another mat with a floral design)
- Concertina card lined with baking (parchment) or greaseproof paper
- Clear alcohol (optional)

Spread the cake lace mix into the butterflies and flower lace mats, and place them in the oven to dry, following the manufacturer's instructions (see Cake Lace).

A

Remove the butterflies from the mat first, carefully bend them in half down the middle and press them into the concertina card to give them shape (A). Leave them to finish drying or return them to the oven on a metal tray if it's particularly humid. If the butterflies curl slightly, try to straighten the wings before they become too brittle.

Cut out the flowers from the floral mat design and stick them onto the cupcake, either using edible glue or by brushing some clear alcohol or water onto the cupcake first. Finally, stick the shaped butterflies onto the cupcake with more edible glue.

Recipes and Techniques

CAKE RECIPES

Always source the finest ingredients for a superior flavour and to ensure your cakes taste as amazing as they look. Bake your cakes in a tin that is 2.5cm (1in) larger than the required final dimensions to achieve a professional, crust-free finish every time. The sizes and quantities specified in the charts that follow in this section will produce cakes that are about 7.5–9cm (3–3½in) deep. Use smaller quantities to bake shallower cakes and mini cakes (see Mini Cakes).

Measuring in Cups

If you prefer to use US cup measurements, please use the following conversions:

Liquid

- 1 tsp = 5ml
- 1 tbsp = 15ml (or 20ml for Australia)
- ½ cup = 120ml/4fl oz
- 1 cup = 240ml/8½fl oz

Caster (superfine) sugar/brown sugar

- ½ cup = 100g/3½oz
- 1 cup = 200g/7oz

Butter

- 1 tbsp = 15g/½oz
- 2 tbsp = 25g/1oz
- ½ cup/1 stick = 115g/4oz
- 1 cup/2 sticks = 225g/8oz

Icing (confectioners') sugar

- 1 cup = 115g/4½oz

Flour

- 1 cup = 125g/4½oz

Sultanas (golden raisins)

- 1 cup = 165g/5¾oz

PREPARING CAKE TINS

To prevent your cake from sticking to the baking tin (pan) I prefer to line the bottom and sides of the tin well before adding the cake mixture and baking.

1 To line the bottom of round cake tins, lay your tin on a piece of greaseproof paper or baking (parchment) paper and draw around it using an edible pen. Using scissors, cut around the inside of the line so that the circle will be a good fit, and put aside. Cut a long strip of the paper at least 9cm (3½in) wide, fold one of the long sides over by 1cm (⅜in) and crease firmly, then open out. Cut slits from the edge nearest to the fold up to the fold, with each slit about 2.5cm (1in) apart. Put the strip around the inside of tin, with the fold tucked into the bottom corner, then add the greaseproof paper circle and smooth down.

2 For square cakes, lay a piece of greaseproof or baking (parchment) paper over the top of the tin. Cut a square that overlaps it on each side by 7.5cm (3in). Cut a slit at each end on two opposite sides. Push the paper inside the tin and tuck the flaps behind.

CAKE PORTION GUIDE

The following chart indicates approximately how many portions will be made by the different cake sizes. The number specified is based on each portion being about 2.5cm (1in) square and 9cm (3½in) deep.

Size	10cm (4in)		13cm (5in)		15cm (6in)		18cm (7in)		20cm (8in)		23cm (9in)		25cm (10in)		28cm (11in)	
Shape	O	Sq	O	Sq	O	Sq	O	Sq	O	Sq	O	Sq	O	Sq	O	Sq
Portions	5	10	10	15	20	25	30	40	40	50	50	65	65	85	85	100

CLASSIC SPONGE CAKE

I have used one basic sponge recipe for all the cakes in this book – this classic recipe is so simple to bake and gives great results every time! I have also provided flavour alternatives if you want to vary the taste (see Additional Flavourings). Separate the mixture between two tins to ensure that your sponge cake is really light. If you want to make three layers, split the mixture one-third/two-thirds. For smaller cakes, you can also cut three layers of sponge from a larger square cake. For example, a 15cm (6in) round cake can be cut from a 30cm (12in) square cake (see Note above chart and also Layering, Filling and Preparation).

Tip

Ensure that your butter and eggs are at room temperature before you start.

1 Preheat your oven to 160°C/325°F/Gas Mark 3 and line your tins (pans) (see Preparing Cake Tins).

2 In a large electric mixer, beat the butter and sugar together until light and fluffy. Add the eggs gradually, beating well between each addition, then add the flavouring.

3 Sift the flour, add to the mixture and mix very carefully until just combined.

4 Remove the bowl from the mixer and fold the mixture through gently with a spatula to finish. Tip the mixture into your prepared tin or tins and spread with a palette knife or the back of a spoon.

5 Bake in the oven until a skewer inserted into the centre of your cakes comes out clean. The baking time will vary depending on your oven. Check small cakes after 20 minutes and larger cakes after 40 minutes.

6 Leave to cool, then wrap the cake in cling film (plastic wrap) and refrigerate until ready to use.

DEEPER CAKES

For deeper cakes, simply bake up to one and a half times the recipe. You may need to bake this in two batches if you only have a couple of tins. Leave the cakes to cool slightly before turning them out and refilling the tins with the mixture.

SHELF LIFE

Sponges should be made up to 24 hours in advance. Freeze them if they are not being used the next day. After the one to two day processes of layering and covering the cakes, the finished cakes should last for up to three to four days out of the fridge.

Note: If cutting three layers from a larger square cake: for a 15cm (6in) round cake, bake an 8 egg/400g (14oz) butter etc. mix in a 30cm (12in) square tin; for a 13cm (5in) round or square cake, bake a 7 egg/350g (12oz) mix in a 28cm (11in) square tin; for a 10cm (4in) round or square cake, bake a 6 egg/300g (10½oz) mix in a 25cm (10in) square tin. Add five to ten per cent extra flour for deeper tiers and carved cakes, or if you find that your sponges are too soft to work with.

Cake size: round / square	13cm (5in) / 10cm (4in)	15cm (6in) / 13cm (5in)	18cm (7in) / 15cm (6in)	20cm (8in) / 18cm (7in)	23cm (9in) / 20cm (8in)	25cm (10in) / 23cm (9in)	28cm (11in) / 25cm (10in)	30cm (12in) / 28cm (11in)	33cm (13in) / 30cm (12in)	35cm (14in) / 33cm (13in)
Unsalted butter	150g (5½oz)	200g (7oz)	250g (9oz)	325g (11½oz)	450g (1lb)	525g (1lb 3oz)	650g (1lb 7oz)	800g (1lb 12oz)	1kg (2lb 4oz)	1.25kg (2lb 12oz)
Caster (superfine) sugar	150g (5½oz)	200g (7oz)	250g (9oz)	325g (11½oz)	450g (1lb)	525g (1lb 3oz)	650g (1lb 7oz)	800g (1lb 12oz)	1kg (2lb 4oz)	1.25kg (2lb 12oz)
Medium eggs	3	4	5	6	9	10	12	14	18	22
Vanilla extract (tsp)	½	1	1	1½	2	2	2½	4	5	6
Self-raising (-rising) flour	150g (5½oz)	200g (7oz)	250g (9oz)	325g (11½oz)	450g (1lb)	525g (1lb 3oz)	650g (1lb 7oz)	800g (1lb 12oz)	1kg (2lb 4oz)	1.25kg (2lb 12oz)

ADDITIONAL FLAVOURINGS

Lemon Add the finely grated zest of one lemon per 100g (3½oz) of sugar.

Orange Add the finely grated zest of two oranges per 250g (9oz) of sugar.

Chocolate Replace 15g (½oz) of flour with 15g (½oz) of cocoa powder (unsweetened cocoa) per 100g (3½oz) of flour.

Banana Replace the caster (superfine) sugar with brown sugar. Add one mashed overripe banana and ½ teaspoon mixed spice (apple pie spice) per 100g (3½oz) of flour.

Coffee and walnut Replace 15g (½oz) of flour with 15g (½oz) of finely chopped walnuts per 100g (3½oz) of flour. Replace the caster sugar with brown sugar and add cooled shots of espresso coffee to taste.

COCONUT AND LIME CAKE

This is my newest favourite recipe, which I have adapted slightly since I discovered it originally, and had to include in this book! The fresh zesty flavour of the cake makes a fabulous, more exotic alternative to the classic recipes we are familiar with.

it's slightly more crumbly in texture due to the desiccated coconut so make sure the cake is nice and cold when working with it and use a good sharp serrated knife. I like to use buttercream for the filling but would suggest coating the outside of the cake with white ganache to seal in the crumbs and give a good firm surface to ice onto.

MATERIALS

Makes a 13cm (5in) round cake, or 10 cupcakes.

- 1 lime
- 125g (4½oz) unsalted butter
- 125g (4½oz) caster (superfine) sugar
- 30g (1oz) desiccated (dry unsweetened shredded) coconut
- 15ml (1 tbsp) milk
- 2 eggs
- 140g (5oz) self-raising (-rising) flour
- ½ tsp baking powder

1 Zest the lime and place in the bowl of an electric mixer, together with the butter and sugar.

2 Juice the lime and combine in another small bowl with the coconut and milk. Set aside to soak.

3 Cream the butter mix until pale and fluffy before adding the eggs one at a time, mixing well between each addition.

4 Add the flour and baking powder and mix until partially combined.

5 Add the coconut mixture and continue mixing everything until combined. Do not over-mix.

Tip

For layering, use lime syrup with Malibu to taste and lime buttercream.

Note: To adapt the recipe to make different sizes, multiply the ingredients, as follows:

Cake size (round)	13cm (5in)	15cm (6in)	18cm (7in)	20cm (8in)	23cm (9in)	25cm (10in)	28cm (11in)	30cm (12in)	33cm (13in)	35cm (14in)
Multiplier	1	1.25	1.75	2.25	3	3.5	4.25	5.25	6.5	8

RED VELVET CAKE

Red velvet cake originated in South America and has been a very popular choice of wedding and celebration cake throughout the US ever since, becoming popular in the UK and other countries in the last few years. As the name suggests, it is a red or red-brown coloured cake, coloured with red food colouring (or beetroot; a natural food colouring) and cocoa powder. It is often filled with either cream cheese or buttercream frosting.

I use a mixture of white chocolate ganache and vanilla buttercream for my red velvet cake. I coat the cake in the ganache mix to give it a nice firm surface before covering it with sugarpaste/fondant to give the cake a longer shelf life, removing the need to keep it in the fridge once iced.

MATERIALS

Makes a 15cm (6in) square or 18cm (7in) round cake, or 16 cupcakes.

- 20ml (1½ tbsp) strained lemon juice
- 225ml (8 fl oz) milk
- 125g (4½oz) unsalted butter
- 300g (10½oz) caster (superfine) sugar
- 2 eggs
- 25g (1oz) cocoa powder (unsweetened cocoa)
- 2 tsp red paste food colouring (I use Sugarflair Red Extra)
- 5ml (1 tsp) vanilla extract
- 320g (11¼oz) plain (all-purpose) flour
- ½ tsp salt
- 1 tsp bicarbonate of soda (baking soda)

1 Drop 10ml (2 tbsp) of lemon juice into the milk. Don't panic – it will curdle!

2 Cream the butter and sugar together in an electric mixer until pale and soft.

3 Add the eggs one at a time, mixing well between each addition.

4 In a small bowl, make a paste with half the cocoa powder, food colouring, vanilla extract and enough of the milk mixture to make a fairly loose paste. Ensure all the ingredients are perfectly blended and smooth.

5 Add about three tablespoons of the butter, sugar and egg mixture to the paste, mix and stir well to combine until perfectly smooth. Now tip everything back into the mixer and mix again to combine.

6 Slowly add half the rest of the milk, then half the flour mixed with the remaining cocoa powder. Now add the rest of the milk and the remaining flour and cocoa powder.

7 Finish by adding the salt, bicarbonate of soda and remaining lemon juice.

Tip

As for the other sponge cakes, bake the cake an inch bigger than you need and trim off the crust.

Note: To adapt the recipe to make different sizes, multiply the ingredients, as follows:

Cake size (round)	13cm (5in)	15cm (6in)	18cm (7in)	20cm (8in)	23cm (9in)	25cm (10in)	28cm (11in)	30cm (12in)	33cm (13in)	35cm (14in)
Multiplier	0.5	0.75	1	1.25	1.75	2.0	2.75	3.5	4.75	6

FILLINGS AND COVERINGS

Fillings give moisture and flavour to a cake. Your choice of filling should complement the type or flavour of your sponge: the most versatile are buttercream and ganache, with ganache generally used for chocolate-covered cakes. Use these recipes on cakes at room temperature and don't refrigerate them until they are ready to serve. Fillings can be used to seal and coat cakes, cover gaps, correct imperfections and create a firm, smooth surface for icing.

BUTTERCREAM

Makes about 500g (1lb 2oz); enough for an 18–20cm (7–8in) round or square layered cake, or 20–24 cupcakes.

MATERIALS

- 225g (8oz) unsalted or slightly salted butter, softened
- 275g (9¾oz) icing (confectioners') sugar
- 15ml (1 tbsp) water
- 5ml (1 tsp) vanilla extract or alternative flavouring

EQUIPMENT

- Large electric mixer
- Spatula

1 Place the butter and icing sugar in the bowl of a large electric mixer and mix together, starting on a low speed to prevent the mixture from going everywhere.

2 Add the water and vanilla or other flavouring and increase the speed, beating the buttercream really well until it is pale, light and fluffy.

3 Store for up to two weeks in an airtight container in the fridge.

SUGAR SYRUP

Sugar syrup can be brushed onto sponge to enhance its flavour and make it moist. Use according to its taste or texture – be careful not to use too much or the sponge will become overly sweet and sticky.

Makes enough for a 20cm (8in) layered, round cake (a square cake will need slightly more), 25 fondant fancies, or 20–24 cupcakes.

MATERIALS

- 85g (3oz) caster (superfine) sugar
- 80ml (5½ tbsp) water
- 5ml (1 tsp) vanilla extract (optional)

EQUIPMENT

- Saucepan
- Metal spoon

1 Bring the sugar and water to the boil, stirring once or twice. Add the vanilla extract, if using, and leave to cool.

2 Store for up to one month in an airtight container in the fridge.

Lemon, lime or orange flavour Replace the water with freshly squeezed, finely-strained lemon or lime, or orange juice. You can also add a little lemon-, lime- or orange-flavoured liqueur (to taste) to heighten the citrusy tang.

GANACHE

This luxuriously rich, silky smooth filling is made from chocolate and cream. Ganache sets firmer than buttercream at room temperature, so it gives the cake a firm surface to ice on, resulting in sharper, cleaner edges and angles. Always use good quality chocolate with at least a 53 per cent cocoa solids content.

Makes about 500g (1lb 2oz); enough for an 18–20cm (7–8in) round or square layered cake, or 20–24 cupcakes.

MATERIALS
- 300g (10½oz) plain (semisweet or bittersweet) chocolate, chopped, or callets
- 200g (7oz) double (heavy) cream

EQUIPMENT
- Saucepan
- Mixing bowl
- Spatula

1 Place the chocolate in a bowl.

2 Bring the cream to the boil in a saucepan, then pour it over the chocolate. Stir until the chocolate has completely melted and is perfectly combined with the cream.

3 Leave to cool and then cover and store in the fridge. It will keep refrigerated for up to one week.

Ensure that your ganache or buttercream is at room temperature before you use it – you may even need to warm it slightly before spreading.

White Chocolate Ganache

White chocolate ganache is a sumptuous filling for heavy sponge cakes (those that have been made with extra flour) and makes an ideal alternative to buttercream. Simply follow the ganache recipe (see Ganache) but use 150g (5½oz) cream to 350g (12oz) white chocolate. If you are making a small batch, melt the white chocolate before mixing it with the hot cream.

BAKING AND COVERING TECHNIQUES

LAYERING, FILLING AND PREPARATION

To achieve smooth, neatly shaped, professional-looking cakes every time, it is essential to prepare your cakes in the right way, ready for icing. Sponge cakes usually consist of two, three or four layers (see Classic Sponge Cake) and are filled and coated with buttercream or ganache before being iced with sugarpaste (rolled fondant).

MATERIALS

- Buttercream or ganache (see Fillings and Coverings) for filling and covering
- Sugar syrup (see Fillings and Coverings) for brushing
- Jam (jelly) or conserve (preserves), for filling (optional)

EQUIPMENT

- Cake leveller
- Large serrated knife
- Ruler
- Small sharp paring knife (optional)
- Cake board, plus chopping board or large cake board if needed
- Turntable
- Palette knives
- Pastry brush

1 Cut the dark-baked crust from the base of your cakes. If you have two sponges of equal depths, use a cake leveller to cut them to the same height. If you have baked one-third of your cake mixture in one tin and two-thirds in the other, cut two layers from the deeper sponge with a large serrated knife or cake leveller to make three layers. Alternatively, cut three layers from a larger square cake: cut a round from two opposite quarters of the square close to the corners for two layers, then a semi-circle from the other two opposite quarters and piece together for the third layer. Your finished cake will be on a 1.25cm (½in) cake board, so the height of your layers together should be about 9cm (3½in) deep.

2 You should have either baked your cake 2.5cm (1in) larger all around than required or baked a larger sponge (see Classic Sponge Cake). Cut around your cake board (this will be the size of your cake), cutting straight down without angling the knife inwards or outwards. For round cakes, use a small sharp paring knife to do this and for square cakes use a large serrated one.

3 Place your three layers of sponge together to check that they are all even and level, trimming away any sponge if necessary. Place your base cake board on a turntable. If the board is smaller than the turntable, put a chopping board or another large cake board underneath. Use a non-slip mat if necessary.

4 Using a medium-sized palette knife, spread a small amount of buttercream or ganache onto the cake board and stick down your bottom layer of sponge. Brush sugar syrup over the cake – the quantity will depend upon how moist you want your cake to be.

5 Spread an even layer of buttercream or ganache about 3mm (⅛in) thick over the sponge, then a thin layer of jam or conserve, if using any. Repeat this procedure for the next

layer. Try not to add too much filling between the layers of sponge, as the cake will sink slightly under the weight of the icing and ridges will appear. Finish by adding the top layer and brushing with more sugar syrup.

6 Cover the sides of the cake in buttercream or ganache, then the top – you only need a very thin, even layer. If the coating becomes 'grainy' as it picks up cake crumbs, place it in the fridge for about 15 minutes to set and then add a thin second coat. This undercoat is referred to as a 'crumb coat' and helps to seal the sponge.

7 Refrigerate your prepared cake for 20 minutes– 1 hour to firm it up, before attempting to cover it with icing or marzipan.

FILLING AND COVERING QUANTITIES

Size	10cm (4in)	13cm (5in)	15cm (6in)	18cm (7in)	20cm (8in)	23cm (9in)	25cm (10in)	28cm (11in)
Buttercream or ganache	175g (6oz)	250g (9oz)	350g (12oz)	500g (1lb 2oz)	650g (1lb 7oz)	800g (1lb 12oz)	1.1kg (2lb 7oz)	1.25kg (2lb 12oz)

COVERING WITH SUGARPASTE

Before icing your cake, cover it with a smooth buttercream or ganache layer to conceal any imperfections that would otherwise be visible. You can cover cakes with a second coat of icing if necessary, or cover with a layer of marzipan before you ice it.

ROUND CAKES

MATERIALS
- Sugarpaste (rolled fondant)
- Icing (confectioners') sugar, for dusting (optional)

EQUIPMENT
- Greaseproof paper or baking (parchment) paper
- Scissors
- Large non-stick rolling pin
- Large non-stick board with non-slip mat (optional)
- Icing and marzipan spacers
- Needle scriber
- Icing smoother
- Small sharp knife

1 Cut a piece of greaseproof/baking paper 7.5cm (3in) larger around than your cake. Place your cake on top.

2 Knead the sugarpaste until soft. Roll it out with the rolling pin either onto the board or a work-surface dusted with icing (confectioners') sugar if the paste is sticky. Use the spacers to obtain the correct width – about 4mm (¼in). Lift the sugarpaste up with a rolling pin and turn it a quarter turn before laying it down to roll again. Try to keep it in a round shape to fit over your cake easily. Push out any air bubbles, or use a needle scriber to burst them.

3 With a rolling pin, pick up and lay the sugarpaste over the cake. Use your hands to smooth it around and down the sides. Pull the sugarpaste away from the sides to unpleat the pleats as you go until you reach the base.

4 Go over the top of the cake with a smoother in a circular motion. For the sides, work around the cake in forward circular movements, almost cutting the excess paste at the base. Trim the excess with a sharp knife. Smooth the cake one final time to ensure a perfect finish.

CAKE COVERING QUANTITIES

Note: Allow slightly more for square and octagonal cakes.

Cake size (9cm/3½in deep)	15cm (6in)	18cm (7in)	20cm (8in)	23cm (9in)	25cm (10in)	28cm (11in)
Marzipan/sugarpaste (rolled fondant)	650g (1lb 7oz)	750g (1lb 10oz)	850g (1lb 14oz)	1kg (2lb 4oz)	1.25kg (2lb 12oz)	1.5kg (3lb 5oz)

SQUARE OR OCTAGONAL CAKES

Icing a square or octagonal cake is done in much the same way as a round cake. However, you must be careful with the corners to prevent the icing from tearing. Gently cup the icing in your hands around the corners before you start working it down the sides of the cake. Any tears in the icing can be mended with clean soft icing, but do this as soon as possible so that it blends in well.

To achieve a sharper edge around the cake use two smoothers to tease the icing almost to a point. Work fairly quickly in sections around the cake. Ganache-coated cakes work best as they stay firm while you are working. You can always fill with buttercream and coat using white ganache for pale iced cakes!

SECURING RIBBON AROUND CAKES AND BOARDS

To secure ribbon around the base of a cake, first measure how long the ribbon needs to be by wrapping it around the cake so that it overlaps by about 1cm (⅜in). Trim to length with a sharp pair of scissors. Attach double-sided tape to either end of the ribbon on the same side. Stick one end directly in place onto the icing, then wrap the ribbon around the cake and stick the other end, overlapping, onto the first end. For square cakes, put the double-sided tape around each corner as well as a small piece in the centre of each side.

For professional results, attach double-faced satin ribbon around the edge of the cake board in a matching or complementary colour. Use 1.5cm (⅝in) wide ribbon and secure at intervals around the board with double-sided tape.

ICING CAKE BOARDS

For a clean, professional finish to your cake, cover the base cake board with icing.

1 Moisten the board with some water. Roll out the sugarpaste (rolled fondant) to 4mm (⅛in) thick, ideally using icing or marzipan spacers. Place the board either on a turntable or bring it towards the edge of the work surface. Pick the icing up on the rolling pin and lay it over the cake board so that it is hanging down over it.

2 Use your icing smoother in a downward motion to cut a smooth edge around the board. Cut away any excess icing. Finish by smoothing the top, using circular movements to achieve a flat and perfectly smooth surface for your cake to sit on. Leave to dry overnight.

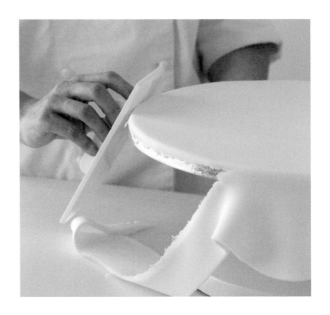

CAKE BOARD COVERING QUANTITIES

Cake board size	23cm (9in)	25cm (10in)	28cm (11in)	30cm (12in)	33cm (13in)	35.5cm (14in)
Sugarpaste (rolled fondant)	600g (1lb 5oz)	650g (1lb 7oz)	725g (1lb 9½oz)	850g (1lb 14oz)	1kg (2lb 4oz)	1.2kg (2lb 10½oz)

PIPING WITH SLUDGE

Sometimes when stacking cakes we are left with a small gap between the bottom of a tier and the top of the next. This can be filled with royal icing, which you may need to colour first to match the sugarpaste/fondant, or you can use sludge!

Sludge is sugarpaste (rolled fondant), softened with water to a paste consistency. It can be placed into a piping bag, just like royal icing, and piped into any gaps. You can either use your finger or a damp paintbrush to remove the excess and create a smooth join. Sludge is also useful for filling in any dents, holes and pinpricks left in the icing anywhere on the cake. Make sure the icing on the cake is dry first: it is best to pipe sludge the following day when decorating the cake.

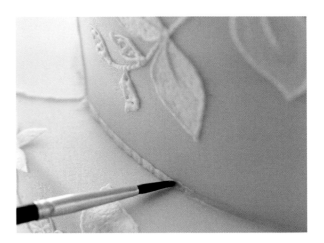

ASSEMBLING TIERED CAKES

Stacking cakes to create a series of tiers is a fairly simple process, but you need to follow the correct procedure to ensure that the structure of the cake is firm and reliable. I advise using hollow plastic dowels because they are sturdy and easy to cut to the correct height. Thinner plastic dowels or even large strong straws are suitable for smaller cakes. See the chart below as a guide to the number of dowels you will need.

MATERIALS

- Iced cake board (see Icing Cake Boards)
- Stiff royal icing (see Royal Icing Recipe)

EQUIPMENT

- Cake top marking template
- Needle scriber or marking tool
- Hollow plastic dowels
- Edible pen
- Large serrated knife
- Spare cake board
- Spirit level
- Icing smoothers

1 Use the cake top marking template to find the centre of your base cake.

2 Using a needle scriber or marking tool, mark the cake where the dowels should go. These need to be positioned well inside the diameter of the cake to be stacked on top. Push a dowel into the cake where it has been marked. Using an edible pen, mark the dowel where it meets the top of the cake.

3 Remove the dowel and cut it at the mark with a large serrated knife. Cut the other dowels to the same height and insert into the cake. Place a cake board on top of the dowels and check that they are equal in height by using a spirit level on the board.

4 Stick your base cake onto the centre of the iced cake board with stiff royal icing. Use your smoothers to move it into position if necessary. Leave the icing to set for a few minutes before stacking on the next tier. Repeat to attach a third tier if needed.

DOWEL QUANTITIES

Cake size	15cm (6in)	20cm (8in)	25cm (10in)
No. of dowels	3–4	3–4	4–5

MINI CAKES

Mini cakes are small round or square cakes that are cut from a large square cake then layered, filled and iced in a similar way as full-size cakes. The number and size of cakes you want will determine the size of the large cake, but it is best to opt for one slightly larger than your requirements to allow for wastage. I make my square mini cakes 5cm (2in), so to make nine you will need an 18cm (7in) square cake. Refer to the charts in the Cake Recipes section, but use only two-thirds of the ingredient quantities, as mini cakes are shallower. Bake all the mixture in one tin (pan) rather than dividing it between two as you would for a larger cake.

MATERIALS
- Large square baked classic sponge cake (see Cake Recipes)
- Sugar syrup (see Fillings and Coverings)
- Buttercream or ganache (see Fillings and Coverings)
- Sugarpaste (rolled fondant)

EQUIPMENT
- Cake leveller
- Circle cutter or serrated knife
- Pastry brush
- Cake cards (optional)
- Palette knife
- Large non-stick rolling pin
- Large non-stick board with non-slip mat
- Metal ruler
- Large sharp knife
- Large circle cutter or small sharp knife
- Two icing smoothers

MINIATURE ROUND CAKES

1 Slice your large square cake horizontally into two even layers using a cake leveller. Cut small individual rounds with a cutter.

2 Brush the pieces of sponge with sugar syrup and sandwich together with either buttercream (plus jam (jelly) if desired) or ganache if using a chocolate-flavoured cake. It's easier if you stick the bottom piece of cake to a cake card the same size and shape as your mini cake using buttercream or ganache, but not essential. Working quickly, pick up each cake and cover the sides evenly with buttercream or ganache. Finish by covering the top and then place the cakes in the fridge for at least 20 minutes to firm up.

Tip

You will find it easier to work with sponge if it's very cold, as it will be much firmer.

3 Roll out a 38cm (15in) square, 5mm (¼in) thick piece of sugarpaste with a large non-stick rolling pin on a large non-stick board set over a non-slip mat. Cut nine small squares and lay one over each cake. If you are a beginner, prepare half the cakes at a time, keeping the other squares under cling film (plastic wrap) to prevent them from drying out.

4 Use your hands to work the icing down around the sides of the cake and trim away the excess with a large circle cutter.

5 Use two icing smoothers on either side of the cake, going forwards and backwards and turning the cake as you go, to create a perfectly smooth result. Leave the icing to dry, ideally overnight, before decorating the cakes.

Miniature Square Cakes

Square mini cakes are created in a similar way to the round ones, so follow the instructions for Miniature Round Cakes. Cut out squares of cake using a serrated knife, and use a sharp knife to cut away the excess icing around the sides. Finish the cakes by using smoothers on opposite sides to press and smooth the icing around the four sides.

BAKING CUPCAKES

To bake the cupcakes in this book follow the Classic Sponge Cake recipe used for the full-size cakes. To make a batch of 10–12 cupcakes, use the quantities given for a 13cm (5in) round or 10cm (4in) square cake.

To bake the mixture, place cupcake cases (liners) in tartlet tins (pans) or muffin trays (pans) and fill them two-thirds to three-quarters full. Bake in a preheated oven at 180°C/350°F/Gas Mark 4 for about 20 minutes, until the cakes are springy to touch.

I prefer to use plain foil cupcake cases, available in a range of colours, because the foil keeps the cakes fresh, and there is no pattern to draw attention away from the decoration on the cakes. But they also come in plain or patterned paper, and you can use decorative cases for plainer cupcakes.

COVERING CUPCAKES WITH SUGARPASTE

Sugarpaste (rolled fondant)-covered cupcakes are quick and easy to make. Simply use a cutter to cut out a circle of sugarpaste and place it inside the cupcake top. Use cupcakes that have a nice even, slightly domed shape, and trim them if necessary.

1 Using a palette knife, spread a thin layer of flavoured buttercream or ganache over the cupcakes to form a perfectly rounded, smooth surface for the icing to sit on.

2 Roll out some sugarpaste and, using a circle cutter, cut out circles that are very slightly bigger than the cupcake top. I would suggest cutting out nine at a time and covering any circles that you are not using with cling film (plastic wrap). Cover the cupcakes one at a time, using the palm of your hand to drape the icing out to the edges to completely cover the tops of the cupcakes.

BAKING COOKIES

Cookies also give you plenty of creative scope, as you can cut all manner of shapes from the dough and decorate them in many different ways to suit every occasion. They offer an ideal opportunity to involve children and have some fun with their preparation. For added convenience, cookies can be made well in advance of an event.

SHELF LIFE

The cookie dough can be made a few days ahead or stored in the freezer until ready to use. The baked cookies will keep for up to one month.

MATERIALS

- 250g (9oz) unsalted butter
- 250g (9oz) caster (superfine) sugar
- 1–2 medium eggs
- 5ml (1 tsp) vanilla extract
- 500g (1lb 2oz) plain (all-purpose) flour, plus extra for dusting

EQUIPMENT

- Large electric mixer
- Spatula
- Deep tray or plastic container
- Rolling pin
- Cookie cutters or templates
- Sharp knife (if using templates)
- Baking trays (sheets) lined with greaseproof paper or baking (parchment) paper

1 In a large electric mixer, beat the butter and sugar together until creamy and quite fluffy.

2 Add the eggs and vanilla extract and mix until they are well combined.

3 Sift the flour into the mixer bowl and mix until all the ingredients just come together. You may need to do this in two stages – do not overmix.

4 Tip the dough into a container lined with cling film (plastic wrap) and press down firmly. Cover with cling film and refrigerate for at least 30 minutes.

5 On a work surface lightly dusted with flour, roll out the cookie dough to 4mm (⅛in) thick. Sprinkle a little extra flour on top of the dough as you roll to prevent it from sticking – don't add too much or your cookies will be dry.

6 Cut out your shapes either with cutters or using templates and a sharp knife. Place on baking trays lined with greaseproof or baking paper and return to the fridge to rest for at least 30 minutes. Meanwhile, preheat your oven to 180°C/350°F/Gas Mark 4.

7 Bake the cookies for about 10 minutes, depending on their size, or until they are golden brown. Leave them to cool completely before storing them in an airtight container until you are ready to decorate them.

ADDITIONAL FLAVOURINGS

Chocolate Substitute 50g (1¾oz) flour with cocoa powder (unsweetened cocoa).
Citrus Omit the vanilla and add the finely grated zest of one lemon or orange.
Almond Replace the vanilla with 5ml (1 tsp) almond extract.

DECORATING TECHNIQUES

ROYAL ICING RECIPE

Royal icing is such a versatile medium, as it can be used for icing cakes and cookies, intricately piping decorations or for simply attaching and sticking. Learning to work with royal icing is a one of the most important skills to acquire in cake decorating.

For best results, use royal icing while it is as fresh as possible. However, it will keep for up to five days when stored an airtight container. If it is not used immediately, re-beat the mixture back to its correct consistency before use.

MATERIALS
- 2 medium egg whites or 15g (½oz) dried egg albumen powder mixed with 75ml (5 tbsp) water
- 500g (1lb 2oz) icing (confectioners') sugar

EQUIPMENT
- Large electric mixer
- Sieve (strainer)
- Spatula

1 If using dried egg powder, soak it in the water for at least 30 minutes in advance, but ideally overnight in the fridge.

2 Sift the icing sugar into the bowl of a large electric mixer and add the egg whites or strained reconstituted egg mixture.

3 Mix together on a low speed for about 3–4 minutes until the icing has reached a stiff-peak consistency – this is needed for attaching decorations and gluing cakes together.

4 Store the icing in an airtight container covered with a damp, clean cloth to prevent it from drying out.

Soft-Peak Royal Icing

You may need to add a tiny amount of water to your royal icing to soften it slightly so that it pipes easily. When you pull up the icing, peaks should form and softly and slowly collapse down, rather than staying upright.

MAKING A PIPING BAG

1 Cut two equal triangles from a large square of greaseproof paper or baking (parchment) paper. As a guide, cut from a 15–20cm (6–8in) square for small piping (pastry) bags and from a 30–35.5cm (12–14in) square for large piping bags.

2 If you are right-handed, keep the centre point towards you with the longest side farthest away and curl the right-hand corner inwards. Bring the point to meet the centre point. Adjust your hold so the two points are together between right thumb and index finger.

3 With your left hand, curl the left point inwards, bringing it across the front and around to the back of the other two points in the centre. Adjust your grip to hold the three points together with both thumbs and index fingers. Tighten the cone by gently rubbing your thumb and index fingers back and forth to make a sharp tip at the end.

4 Carefully fold the back of the bag (where all the points meet) inwards and press hard along the fold. Repeat to secure. You can make a number of piping bags at a time and put them aside for a decorating session.

PIPING WITH ROYAL ICING

Use soft-peak royal icing (see Royal Icing Recipe) for basic piping work. The size of the tube (tip) you use will depend on the job at hand and how confident you feel.

Fill the piping (pastry) bag until it is no more than one third full. Fold the top over, away from the join, until you have a tight and well-sealed bag. The correct way to hold the piping bag is important. Use your index finger to guide the bag. You can also use your other hand to guide you if it helps.

To pipe dots squeeze the icing out gently until you have the dot that's the size you want. Stop squeezing then lift the bag. If there is a peak in the icing, use a damp brush to flatten it down.

To pipe teardrops once you have squeezed out the dot, pull the tube through the dot, then release the pressure and lift the bag. To pipe elongated teardrops and swirls, squeeze out a ball of icing and drag the icing round to one side to form a swirl or scroll. Increase the pressure and amount of icing you squeeze out for longer, larger shapes. Keeping close to the surface you are piping on is known as 'scratch piping'.

To pipes lines touch the tube down, then lift the bag up in a smooth movement, squeezing gently. Decrease the pressure and touch it back down to the point where you want the line to finish. Try not to drag the icing along, or it will become uneven. Use a template or a cookie outline as a guide where possible.

To pipe a 'snail trail' border squeeze out a large dot of icing and drag the tube (tip) through it to one side, like a teardrop. Repeat this motion around the cake.

ROYAL-ICED COOKIES

This is my preferred method of icing cookies – I love the taste of the crisp white icing against the softer texture of the cookie underneath. Use a squeezable plastic bottle with a small tube instead of piping bags if you are icing a large quantity of cookies.

MATERIALS
- Soft-peak royal icing (see Royal Icing Recipe)

EQUIPMENT
- Small and large piping (pastry) bags (see Making a Piping Bag)
- Piping tubes (tips): nos. 1; 1.5

1 Place the no. 1.5 tube in a small piping bag and fill with soft-peak royal icing. Pipe an outline around the edge of each cookie, or the area that you wish to ice.

2 Thin down some royal icing with water to reach a 'flooding' consistency (test for the desired consistency by lifting your spoon and letting the icing drip back into the bowl – it should remain on the surface for five seconds before disappearing). Place in a large piping bag with a no. 1 tube and 'flood' inside the outlines with icing. For larger cookies, snip off the end of the bag instead of using a tube. To flood a large area, work around the edges of the piped outline and then inwards to the centre to ensure an even covering. Once dry, pipe over any details and stick on decorations as desired.

Making Edible Glue

Edible glue is used for sticking paste items together and onto the cakes. It is easy to make; simply add 40ml (1½fl oz) of cooled boiled water to 0.8ml (⅟₁₆tsp) of CMC. Mix it to dissolve for 10–20 minutes. To thicken the glue, add more CMC; to thin the mixture, add more water.

COVERING COOKIES WITH SUGARPASTE

For neat and professional cookies that are very quick to ice, simply roll out some sugarpaste (rolled fondant) to no more than 3mm (⅛in) thick, then cut out the shape of the cookie with the same cutter or template used for cutting out the cookies from the dough. Stick the cut-out icing shapes onto the cookies using boiled and cooled apricot masking spread or strained jam (jelly), taking care not to stretch or distort the icing.

Templates

All templates are shown at 50% and will need to be enlarged on a photocopier by 200%.
Download full-size printable templates at http://ideas.stitchcraftcreate.co.uk//patterns

DELICATE DOILY ART

PETAL

DESIGNED WITH LOVE

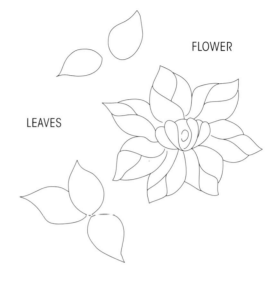

FLOWER

LEAVES

HANNAH'S DAISY LACE
BASIC DAISY LACE DESIGN
Note: sizes may need to be adjusted according
to the exact circumference of the cake.

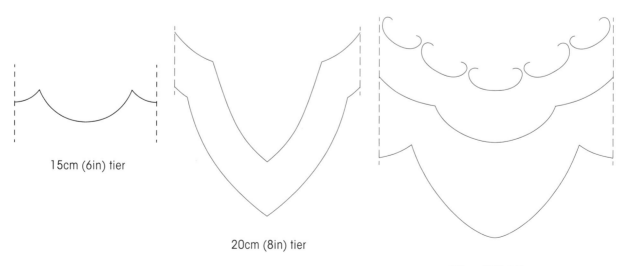

15cm (6in) tier

20cm (8in) tier

25cm (10in) tier

FANCY FLORAL EMBROIDERY
LACE DESIGN

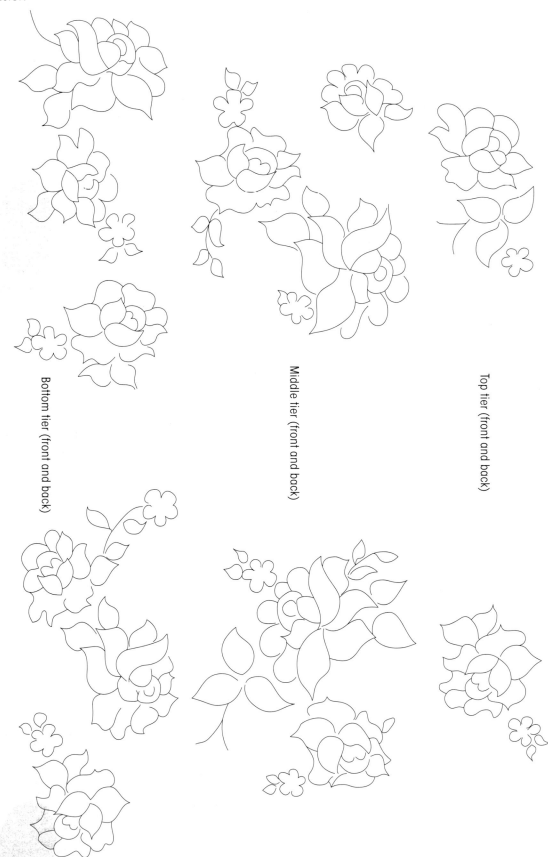

Bottom tier (front and back)

Middle tier (front and back)

Top tier (front and back)

CONTEMPORARY CORDED LACE
CORDED LACE DESIGN

Top tier

PETAL

Bottom tier

ROYAL-ICED BUTTERFLY GARDEN

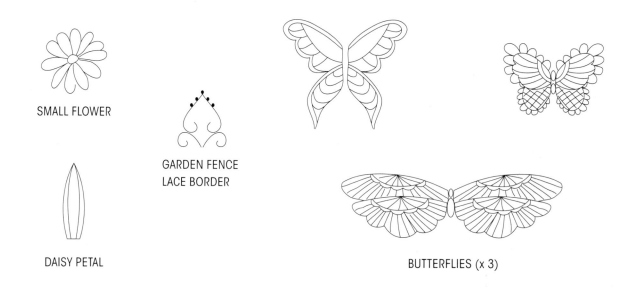

SMALL FLOWER

GARDEN FENCE
LACE BORDER

DAISY PETAL

BUTTERFLIES (x 3)

About the Author

After graduating from the University of Bath with a degree in Foreign Languages, Zoë decided to take a more creative path to follow her true passion of combining art with food and turned to the world of cake decorating. In 2010, she opened The Cake Parlour in south-west London where she designs and creates custom cakes and confections, which often feature in bridal and sugarart titles around the globe, as well as in films and on television. In 2011, Zoë designed a range of cakes for Fortnum and Mason, including a cake for the Queen to celebrate her Diamond Jubilee.

Zoë has published a variety of best-selling books touching on a range of cake creations, from *Chic and Unique Wedding Cakes* to her previous title *Simply Perfect Party Cakes for Kids*. Teaching worldwide, Zoë also imparts her skills and knowledge to individuals through hands-on, intimate sessions and large demonstrations, as well as online via the Craftsy platform.

Acknowledgments

I'd like to thank Mark Scott again for his wonderful imagery and patience with me on the shoots – it can get very hectic at times! I'd also like to thank Beth Dymond for helping with the edit and, as always, my family who are always behind me. A huge thank you too, to one of my favourite wedding venues Fetcham Park (fetchampark.co.uk) who allowed us to shoot some of my cakes against their gorgeous backdrop interior – such a beautiful location. Finally, I'd like to thank all my students, fellow cake-makers and readers for all your enthusiasm, encouragement, help and support. You are all wonderful and inspire me to carry on!

Suppliers

UK

Zoë Clark Cakes
www.zoeclarkcakes.com
Tel: 020 8947 4424

Squires Kitchen
www.squires-shop.com
Tel: 0845 61 71 810

The Cake Decorating Company
www.thecakedecorating company.co.uk
Tel: 0115 969 9800

US

Decorate the Cake
www.decoratethecake.com
Tel: 1-917-382-6653

Global Sugar Art
www.globalsugarart.com
Tel: 1-518-561-3039

AUSTRALIA

Cakes Around Town
www.cakesaroundtown.com.au
Tel: 07 3160 8728

Couture Cakes
www.couturecakes.com.au
Tel: 02 8764 3668

Index

A DAVID & CHARLES BOOK
© F&W Media International, Ltd 2015

David & Charles is an imprint of F&W
Media International, Ltd
Brunel House, Forde Close, Newton
Abbot, TQ12 4PU, UK

F&W Media International, Ltd is a
subsidiary of F+W Media, Inc
10151 Carver Road, Suite #200,
Blue Ash, OH 45242, USA

Text and Designs © Zoë Clark 2015
Layout and Photography © F&W
Media International, Ltd 2015

First published in the UK and USA in 2015

Zoë Clark has asserted her right to be identified
as author of this work in accordance with the
Copyright, Designs and Patents Act, 1988.

ISBN-13: 978-1-4463-0572-0 hardback
ISBN-10: 1-4463-0572-4 hardback

ISBN-13: 978-1-4463-0573-7 paperback
ISBN-10: 1-4463-0573-2 paperback

ISBN-13: 978-1-4463-7073-5 PDF
ISBN-10: 1-4463-7073-9 PDF

ISBN-13: 978-1-4463-7072-8 EPUB
ISBN-10: 1-4463-7072-0 EPUB

Printed in USA by RR Donnelley for:
F&W Media International, Ltd
Brunel House, Forde Close, Newton
Abbot, TQ12 4PU, UK

10 9 8 7 6 5 4 3 2

Content Director: Ame Verso
Editor: Emma Gardner
Project Editor: Beth Dymond
Designer: Jodie Lystor
Photographer: Mark Scott
Production Manager: Beverley Richardson

F+W Media publishes high quality books
on a wide range of subjects.
For more great book ideas visit: www.
stitchcraftcreate.co.uk

Layout of the digital edition of this book may vary
depending on reader hardware and display settings.